TODAY'S INSPIRED LATINA™

Volume VI - Europe Edition

LIFE STORIES OF SUCCESS IN THE FACE OF ADVERSITY

JACQUELINE S. RUIZ
VERONICA SOSA

Today's Inspired Latina

This book is a compilation of stories from numerous Latinas who have each contributed a chapter and is designed to provide inspiration to our readers.

It is sold with the understanding that the publisher and the individual authors are not engaged in the rendering of psychological, legal, accounting or other professional advice. The content and views in each chapter are the sole expression and opinion of its author and not necessarily the views of Fig Factor Media, LLC.

For more information, contact:

Jacqueline S. Ruiz
Fig Factor Media, LLC | www.figfactormedia.com
JJR Marketing, Inc. | www.jjrmarketing.com

Cover Design & Layout by Juan Pablo Ruiz
Printed in the United States of America

ISBN: 978-1-7330635-5-5

Dedicated to Latinas around the world... And the voices and stories within each of them

Contents:

Acknowledgements 6

Introduction 7

Preface 9

PERLA TAMEZ 11

FELISSA ARIAS 23

LYA MARTINEZ 33

ANDREA VILLAMIZAR LÓPEZ 43

ANDREA MESIS-BRUNO 53

DENISE PEDROZA SANDOVAL 63

MYLENE FERNSTRÖM 73

MARIELYS AVILA 83

RUBMARY DÍAZ MARCANO 93

VIRGINIA CALLIZAYA TERCEROS 103

SILVIA TAPIA 113

ESTEFANIA ROA 123

MARITA VALDIZAN 133

BETH MARMOLEJOS 143

ADRIANA MÉNDEZ SNOWDEN 153

ALICIA PONCE-NUÑEZ 163

KARINA ENDULZA 173

LIZBETH RAMIREZ 183

ADRIANA HERNÁNDEZ MARTÍNEZ 193

RENÉE RODRIGUEZ 203

Acknowledgements

Every volume of *Today's Inspired Latina* fills my heart with gratitude, for I know these visions could not be fulfilled without a wonderful, inspired team to help me.

First, to Veronica Sosa, who introduced me to a brave new world of authors with incredible stories and inspiration to share! I hope this collaboration will be the first of many.

I am grateful to the members of my team who have worked tirelessly to make this possible, including the love of my life and business partner, Juan Pablo Ruiz, official series editor Karen Dix, Grizel Morales, Manuel Serna and all who believed in this inspiration from day one.

I'd also like to thank the authors who took part in the maiden voyage of our European version, and all the past authors who continue to lend their support to the mission of *Today's Inspired Latina* and the elevation of a vibrant, author community that perpetuates opportunity, and even bigger dreams. Love to you all!

Introduction

BY JACQUELINE CAMACHO-RUIZ

I'm a big dreamer. But sometimes, your dreams manifest in a bigger way than you could ever imagine! Five years ago, when I first developed the little idea for "*Today's Inspired Latina*," I never imagined that we would be unveiling a sixth volume in Europe in 2019! But it all aligns with the magic that is in my heart, not only for the Latinas in my own country, but those around the world.

It all started when I met Veronica Sosa and she asked me to "cross the pond" to address the Latinas at one of her SHE (Seminars for Hispanic Entrepreneurs in Europe) events. There, completely unexpectedly, I was presented with an award for elevating Latina entrepreneurs in my own country. I knew I had found my European soulmate, a woman whose vision beat in sync with mine for the emerging Latinas of the world. Working together, we could make *Today's Inspired Latina* a global movement. And so we have!

Publishing this book, with so many authors from Europe included in the table of contents, has been a giant leap for the series. In Volume I, we gathered 25 authors from the Chicago area. In the consecutive volumes, we welcomed authors from across the country, and eventually, crossed borders into Mexico and South America. Now we welcome authors from England, Belgium, the Netherlands, Spain, Germany, Sweden, and Italy into our sisterhood of Today's Inspired Latina authors.

Additional volumes are also in production. In 2020, we will

launch two more volumes featuring authors from the United States and one volume of *Today's Inspired Latina* for Latin America, featuring authors from Central and South America, to be launched in Colombia! It's amazing to think that between May 2019 and May 2020, we will have launched four books on three continents! The series is now a full-fledged, international author movement to elevate and inspire Latinas to reach for their dreams, and to never stop, throughout the globe!

To the authors in this volume, I say congratulations, *felicidades, gefeliciteerd, congratulazioni, gratis, and Herzliche Glückwünsche!* I know you will continue the magic, for as long as there are Latinas in the world with stories to tell, voices to be heard, and dreams to be achieved, there will be *Today's Inspired Latina*. Here, there, and everywhere!

Jacqueline S. Ruiz
Entrepreneur, Author, Speaker, Philanthropist, Pilot, Founder of Today's Inspired Latina

Preface

BY VERONICA SOSA

Recently, the world has shifted. There is a rise in new paradigms, based on values. Values which many people believed had disappeared or been discarded. Well, I am celebrating with you today, because those values are returning. It may take time and effort, but slowly, we are claiming them back.

Now is the time when women are taking charge of creating, changing, educating, nurturing, contributing, and campaigning for a better world. A world where we embrace co-creation to build on the magic of love, appreciating what we do and what we have. Creating a better life and world for our children to grow and enjoy harmony.

I feel incredibly humbled and blessed to be a part of this wonderful change of paradigms. I am so grateful that I am a contributor to this change and that I have been given the honor of writing about it in this amazing book. *Today's Inspired Latina Volume VI* is one in the series which gathers together remarkable stories of Latinas from around the world, who have not only encountered adversity, but have conquered it and achieved their goals. It is a great pleasure to introduce these entrepreneurs, mothers, sisters, and daughters whose words will inspire and give courage to others wanting to realize their hopes and dreams.

I am extremely fortunate to be a part of two amazing communities. One of them I founded five years ago here in

Europe. It is called SHE (Seminar for Hispanics Entrepreneurs in Europe) and is an organization for Hispanic women which helps them to achieve their goals and reach their balance between body, mind, and spirit to achieve results and coherence in life. It aspires to provide Latinas on this side of the world with the tools they need to advance their personal and professional lives. We continue to expand globally as we reach out and discover more Latinas needing our help.

The second one is the *Today's Inspired Latina* community, led by my friend and collaborator, Jacqueline Camacho. SHE is very proud to support her movement here in Europe and anywhere else we can. I am so proud to be working with this amazing woman. I admire her not only for her beautiful soul and values but for everything she has achieved, including becoming one of the few Latina pilots in America. I had the good fortune of meeting her through a mutual friend, Steve Gallegos, two years ago. As soon as we met, we both felt a magical connection. Our goals were totally aligned, as we both had a vision to elevate and empower Latina women, and actually, not just Latina women, but all women around the world. My beloved Pilotina and I will support each other all the way!

Although the way we use our individual talents may differ, what is identical is the love we feel in doing it. From Jacqueline's experience in marketing and branding, I have learned about connecting with people and growing relationships through the way you treat them and make them feel. The work we are doing is about nurturing, and while of course, earning money is important, relational capital is equally as important.

Latina power has great recognition throughout the world. We are loud. We are powerful. We are dynamic and unstoppable. We are passionate about everything we do, so when we all collaborate and work in unity, we are able to combine our energies to transform our world to make it a better place to live.

This book will take you on numerous journeys through the stories of Latinas who have become empowered as they have aligned with their creativity and focused on achieving great results in all aspects of their lives. Their words will help you discover how you can overcome obstacles, find the strength to continue, and generate ideas so you too can experience the process, incredible results, and divine magic which comes from co-creation.

I honor you, the reader, and all women with the courage to expose their vulnerability to give others inspiration and create a greater consciousness. In this way, we can all become better, more conscious leaders and continue to grow these new paradigms of greater values.

Seventeen-year-old Tupac Mosley, a homeless graduate who was recently awarded a $3 million dollar scholarship recently said, "Never let your current situation, whatever circumstances you're going through, be a mountain that you can't climb." Remember his words whenever you find yourself in a seemingly hopeless situation.

Challenges and hardships can serve to help us find our path. We may not have a choice in the circumstances we find ourselves, but we can choose how we react to any given situation. Finding self-respect is the first step towards self-development and finding your true potential. Find your inspiration by reading about other people who have made similar journeys. Never be afraid to ask for help. Surround yourself with people who love you and want you to succeed. Take care of yourself and the people around you. It's a balance which can be quite difficult, so you need to take control of your time and make it happen. It's like dancing. Take action to clear your mind and become a better person.

You are a light in this world. Never forget that.

Together is Better. Together we are stronger.

Love,

Veronica

Veronica Sosa
BFM /Foundress of SHE and International Speaker

Perla Tamez

"Be their hero, commit to exceeding their expectations, and the universe will reward you."

Many people have commented on how successful and inspirational I am, even though it is completely natural that I don't see it that way. I just think it is important to believe in yourself and value who you are. When you do not value yourself, you begin to sabotage your own personal, professional, and emotional relationships. You may lower your expectations and take and accept less than what you deserve. You may be treated badly and spiral into depression, with your self-esteem slowly being chipped away until you look back at your life with anguish and pain. You have no reason to accept mistreatment or ever feel like it's deserved.

Bullying behaviors can come from yourself, a partner, a friend, a group of people, your work colleagues, or even your boss. The important thing to remember is that if you are being bullied or mistreated, it is your sole responsibility not to accept it. You have the control to stop it. If you can't do it alone, find help. If someone tells you that you are being abused, listen and act. It's important to identify abuse early and get away so you regain your inner strength and get back on your feet.

Find those in your circle, such as your parents, children, family, spouse, or friends who would bet their lives on you to meet their expectations. Be their hero, commit to exceeding their expectations, and the universe will reward you. There is no other powerful source of support than that.

BUSINESS LESSONS

Growing up, I had a rocky start. My parents came from generations of farmers and immigrated to the U.S. to build a brighter future for their unborn children. As newlyweds, they had jobs, but their prospects in south Texas were limited. During the first years of their marriage, they migrated to Wesley, California to work in the fields. My parents were "fine" with the work but were always looking for the next opportunity. Before I was born, they were struggling to make ends meet, yet they continued to seek ways to become more financially stable. My mother opened a shoe store in Hidalgo, Texas, on the Mexican border, when I was about five years old. She was energetic, a hard worker, and a fighter. She never took "no" for an answer and my dad always supported her. She was always ready to lend a helping hand to anyone in need.

As a young child, my mom would take me to work after school. I learned to socialize with employees and clients. She was always bossing me around to do little things around the store and help the employees with anything they needed. She was trying to keep me busy, but little did she know she was teaching life lessons I would later put to use as a business owner.

From there, my parents ventured into the northern part of Mexico and southern part of the U.S. where we were involved in many businesses, including agriculture, construction development, clothing, dry cleaning, and adult daycare. I continued to go to the office with my mom and learned so much in those years: how to launch a company from the ground up; how to manage people; how important employees are and how they need to be taken care of; how you sometimes have to pitch in to get things done; and how the life of a business owner is unpredictable. You could be leaving the bank in your business suit and receive an emergency call that a giant dry cleaning machine just broke and needs your help to fix it. But the most valuable thing I learned was to have a humble heart and embrace people from all walks of life.

I remember being 14 years old during one hot, 100-degree summer in south Texas, working at the dry cleaners and pressing the clothes with steam raging out of the irons. It felt like an oven. My job that summer was to make hangers and put the logo cover on them. I remember calling the local Mexican radio station to give a shout out to the people at American dry cleaners for handling the heat with a big smile while listening to loud Mexican songs!

Those times were priceless and essential to my entrepreneurial foundation. Success usually does not come fast and easy (like winning the lottery); you must find it. Again, life, work, and duties are your responsibility. Things don't get done for you; if it's your goal, then you must do it.

EMBRACE RESPONSIBILITY, NOT BLAME

I was a 12-year-old rebel about to enter sixth grade. One Friday, I came home and asked my mom for permission to go to the movies with my friends. Immediately, she said "no." In the Mexican culture, you stick with your cousins and at 12 years old, you have no business going to the movies. I was devastated and became upset, then hysterical. The more I tried to convince my mom, the more she refused. I was determined to change her mind so in an effort to make her fold, I told her I wanted to die. I thought the idea might tug at her heart and she'd let me go to the movies.

Instead, she called my bluff and said, "Really? Go ahead!" I had no choice but to soldier on. "I do want to die!" So I ran to the kitchen and got a butter knife and a bottle of Tylenol. I remember crying and yelling at my mother as she failed to give in. Then my dad calmly walked into the room and said, "*Perlucho*, what's going on? You want to kill yourself?" "Yes," I replied, "Because you won't let me go to the movies." He then said to my younger sister, "Poli, bring me the phone. I'm calling the police." He called 911 and I heard him say," Police, can you please come get my daughter. She wants to kill herself and I don't want her to dirty my floor."

Wait, what??

"Dad, please don't do that. It's not true, I don't want to die."

"Well, it's too late. It's your responsibility to talk to the police."

Two or three minutes passed. Then I heard the sirens of the police outside my house and when I peeked out, I saw four police cars with officers ready to keep me from committing suicide. My trick had failed and now I was in this mess and wanted to die of embarrassment. But I had to talk to them. That was the last time I ever tried to manipulate my parents. I was responsible for my life.

THE GOAL THAT DRIVES YOU

When I was 15, I had to cross the international bridge every day to drive me and my sister to school, which was an hour away. My father bought me a brand new, very masculine, Chevrolet truck. He told me that's what I needed so if I ever had an accident, I would be protected. I didn't like my truck, but I had no other choice. A year or so later, he called me and said, "Perla, I have a deal for you. I'm seeing a Cadillac CTS. Do you want it?" "Yes, of course," I replied.

Then he told me, "If I you get this car, it will be the last car we ever give you, but when you get your own vehicle, it has to be the same or better. I don't want to pass you on the expressway and see you driving anything less. To succeed, you must work hard; it doesn't happen magically. It's your responsibility."

I thought to myself, *oh my God, how will I ever do this!* But I took the challenge. That night, they brought home my brand new car, but I couldn't sleep. I was thinking about the huge commitment I had made, wondering how long I would have to keep the car before I could get a better one. I thought to myself, *where there is a will there's a way.* I wouldn't let my parents down for anything. They believed in me.

I graduated from high school in 2005 and started college

in the summer of 2004 while helping at my mom's adult daycare. At the time I had an older boyfriend who was a college graduate and very smart and driven. Following in his footsteps, I graduated high school at the age of 18 with 52 college credits. The summer of 2005, I studied abroad in Spain and had many amazing life experiences.

When I returned, I was determined to graduate as soon as possible and become a speech language pathologist assistant, since I had developed an interest from seeing them treat the elderly at the daycare. I graduated with my bachelor's degree from the University of Texas A & M at the age of 20. It had been a goal that was my responsibility and under my control.

MY COMPANY, MY RESPONSIBILITY

After working nine months on the job as a Speech Language Pathologist Assistant, I decided to invest my time and focus into setting up a small company. My mother connected a phone line directly to my room in my parent's house where Poli served as secretary in her off-time. I leaped into entrepreneurship, knowing my parents had my back.

Next, I returned to Hidalgo, approached an aunt and a close family friend and asked if I could offer my services at their child daycare center. Hidalgo had many underprivileged children who could benefit from speech and occupational therapy. The center opened their doors to me and gave us a 10 x10 space and a closet to store toys and equipment. I happily filled the office with used furniture from my mom, along with dreams of success. I will always be grateful to the ones who gave me my start.

Soon I had a staff and we were all very busy treating patients, but I still continued to work at my first job to cover my licensing fees and operating costs. I was determined to work as hard as I had to, because my therapist colleagues were also betting on my dream. They had left positions at reliable companies to take the leap of faith with me. Eleven years later, those first therapists are still with me.

At the beginning, I lost sleep worrying about failure. But I would convince myself I was on the right path. I would look fear in the eye and grab it by the horns to tell it I'm bigger and better. Now I have become an expert in overcoming fear and embracing it.

A good friend taught me the phrase, "Give a dog a bone to live up to," which means if you set the stage for success, you are indirectly telling that person you believe in them and the person will try harder to become a success. Unknowingly, that's what my parents did with me, trusting that I could succeed. When I didn't know how I was going to succeed, I would find a way.

Within 18 months, I had three large clinics in three cities and in 2010, I had five clinics, 150 employees, and $10 million in revenue. By age 24, I filed my first, personal $1 million tax return!

In my trajectory as an entrepreneur, my family has been at the core of my enterprise. I have opened numerous companies and am now doing private equity investments and engaging international speaking conferences around the globe. Along the way, I married a great man and although our marriage was short-lived, he was a great supporter. We had a baby girl and named her Yvanna Paulette. I am now embracing love and learning the ups and downs of emotional commitments, which are different from job deals.

Find a center of commitment and hold tight to it. If you share the wealth of knowledge, give your kids family values and invest in teaching them that they can be your hero. The investment will pay off!

REFLECTION QUESTIONS

1. How do you show that you take responsibility for your life?

2. Who sets the highest expectations for you and are you living up to them?

3. Which of the "business lessons" that I learned in my story are most important to you?

BIOGRAPHY

Perla Elizabeth Tamez is a visionary serial entrepreneur and licensed speech language pathologist assistant. She has dedicated her life's work to empower others to unlock their true potential. She is also an advocate for healthcare and children's rights policies.

At a very young age, Perla learned to run fiercely in the direction of her dreams. She graduated high school with 52 college hours and at the age of 21, she founded her first outpatient pediatric clinic in 2008, and is now one of the largest providers in southern Texas. She has been at the helm of many startups including a local fashion magazine, staffing company, education enterprise, and real estate firm. Perla is also passionate about politics, international travel, youth outreach, venture capitalism, and the prison rehabilitation system.

In 2014, Perla's unmatched talent was honored with the Small Business Administration Young Entrepreneur of the Year Award for Region VI, representing Arkansas, Louisiana, New Mexico, Oklahoma, and Texas. Today, she is committed to sharing her hard-earned knowledge and experience with others to help them become the best they can be.

Perla looks forward to soon completing her Executive MBA from The University of Texas at Austin.

Perla Tamez
info@perlatamezinspiration.com
Instagram: @Bealovesoldier

Felissa Arias

"The only thing that defines me is what I think about myself."

I grew up in a lower middle-class family in a poor neighborhood in the city of Santo Domingo, Dominican Republic, without advantages, a recognizable last name, or connection to anyone who could help me succeed. Still, I learned that circumstances or surroundings can influence me, but they cannot define who I am. I realized that instead of letting my circumstances keep me down, I can take action and reclaim power over my story. I now know for sure that the only thing that defines me is what I think about myself.

YOUNG ENTREPRENEURSHIP

My mother had a small business selling various articles for school and personal use. When I was seven years old, I watched my mom selling and imagined I could do the same thing! So, I asked her to give me a few pencils, pens, erasers, and pencil sharpeners to sell to my classmates.

At the end of the day, I had sold everything. I paid my mom her share and I was super happy with the profits. I continued to do it, day after day. But it all ended when I discovered that it was illegal to sell merchandise at school. Still, I knew I had a very good future!

My first encounter with business taught me how to earn money, without money, within the rules of the world. After that, I became involved in everything that society told me to do, even when it didn't make sense. It was not exciting, but "I had to do the right thing." I lost myself this way and added a series of limiting beliefs to my mindset that accompanied me through many years of my life.

Life became difficult, complex, and very hard. Many years of anguish, suffering, and doubts passed, without convincing answers to my questions. I felt lost and alone. I fought to earn a living and pay my college tuition. When I was eight, my parents got divorced. Everything in my house was a battle. Often, I sought answers in the wrong places and became involved in toxic relationships.

I started to believe that to win and get what I deserved I would have to work four times harder than the average person. But simultaneously, inside me there was an opposite force, a voice that I tried to silence, that told me not to follow that path. But I continued for many long years without listening to my inner wisdom and following my intuition. I did not know how to face what was happening to me, so I decided to put on my anesthesia mask and keep going on autopilot. I just did what I "had" to do.

I will not lie to you; I felt very desperate and alone, staring into the void with empty pockets. My abilities, efforts, and sacrifices had yielded some fruits, but not enough to flourish and feel successful.

Along the way, I lost myself and become someone who

laughed from the outside and cried on the inside. I did not enjoy my achievements. I felt like a failure, with little pride in myself.

ANOTHER WAY

I began to see everything in life in a fragmented way. I was on one path and my career was on the other; my finances were in ruins because money is only a reflection of our inner self. Since my interior was broken, I could not get my finances in order. When I lost myself, I began to lose everything. In my government career, I was promoted because I worked four times more than the average person. Yet the joy in my life had left. I had attempted, and failed, at several ventures and I wanted a life change because I was not happy with everything that was happening to me, nor anything that I had created.

My hands were tied because I was a slave to my loans and credit card debt and had to live paycheck to paycheck. Some days I had to decide between getting a good meal or putting gas in my car to go to work. Dreaming of a better tomorrow looks great in movies, books, and documentaries, but I didn't think any dreams were possible for me.

In 2013, I was going around in circles, sometimes with small victories, until one day, tired and physically and mentally exhausted, I said to myself, *there has to be another way. Life cannot just be feeling like this until we die.*

That day, a burning desire arose in my heart. I wanted to live a life where I felt full, not empty and lost. I wanted to live a life where I could flourish, not wither, with the passage of time. I decided to stop destroying myself. With every year that passed, a piece of that girl I once was-- so full of enthusiasm that at seven years old she had learned about business and felt happy for her achievements at the end of the day—was fading away. I wanted that joy back!

When I reached rock bottom and could no longer stand my life as it was, an indomitable strength began to surface within me. This strength was accompanied by serenity and serenity brought me clarity. That day, I opened the door to my intuition and to the voice of my soul. I was no longer a fragmented human being; heart and mind began to work together. I stopped being a "human doing" and began a journey to become a human being.

I decided to work on my mindset, an area in my life that needed work, especially since it was responsible for most of the important decisions I made throughout my life. If I wanted freedom of choice, I had to get my mind, habits, and finances in order. From there, I could begin to tell a new story about my life. I committed myself to transforming my finances and in doing so, a new world opened up before my eyes. It was like a rebirth because I beheld a previously unknown, new world of possibilities that once seemed impossible for me.

MORTALITY MOTIVATION

By 2015, I had eliminated all my debts and begun to savor what it meant to live debt-free. I was able to save a considerable sum of money and take the next step towards my professional reinvention. My plan was to become a full-time entrepreneur in a new country. I had lots of ideas, but for some reason, I wanted to continue in my "safety zone" because I had earned my place there, and it is where I thrived.

I thought, after all the sacrifices you have made to get here, now that everything is starting to get better, do you really want to leave and begin a new project that may not be fulfilling? But by mid-2015, plans were put on hold when I had to undergo a complicated surgery. I walked into the clinic for a simple surgical procedure for my endometriosis, expecting a quick recovery. But I woke up in the intensive care room, unable to move. My insides were not what the doctor had expected, and the one-hour surgery had turned into six hours. I received a blood transfusion and was prescribed a month of rest and many treatments before life could return to normal.

At first, the experience was terrifying. But it ultimately led me to reflect even more profoundly on the life I wanted to live. I realized I did not have as much time as I thought, and it gave me the courage to take the step I had been afraid to take for years. I found "mortality motivation" to live with purpose and joy, and no longer postpone anything that I want to do.

Now I saved money, with a date in mind when I would quit my job as budget manager for the Ministry of Foreign Affairs in Dominican Republic and leave everything behind to start over in another country.

A NEW PATH

The first year after moving to Italy was surprisingly difficult.

Every day was new to me and I had to develop a new mindset, habits, and a whole new skillset, because what brings us to point A will not get us to point B.

Suddenly, I found myself back in the fire. I mentally reprogrammed myself to change my old habits and do things differently. Having money in the bank gave me time to think, but it also quickly disappeared. I had to get moving, but this time I wanted to do it with the voice of my soul.

For twenty years I had liked my jobs. They gave me power, recognition, social status, and a good package of benefits. However, they did not give me a sense of fulfillment and self-realization. I made an inventory of my strengths and the tools I had. Then I put a description on paper of what it meant for me to be successful and added how I could leverage my knowledge, professional, and academic experiences.

I put the intention in my heart to reveal the next step to a life where my work fulfilled a greater purpose, in a business that would align with my values and achieve my own version of success. I became more open and ready to share my values and knowledge with the world. I may have often fallen, but I had also often triumphed.

Once we have conquered a challenge, another arises. It is a natural law and necessary for our evolution. A firm commitment to my life purpose emerged in me, along with a desire to use my best talents to heal the world, in accord with the channel of solutions in the universe. My purpose goes hand in hand with serving, which is the universal purpose that we all share; we are all called to serve in different ways.

When we respond to the call of the soul, which knows the path to fullness, we are always connected with the divine grace. We learn to leverage ourselves in our existing earthly tools and are guided by a greater force that sustains us.

I learned that many people may not agree with what you are doing, while the majority who say they understand you, do not. When you have a goal, you may feel alone and can question if the "out of the box" thing you are doing is right. However, I beg you not to stop until you feel full; do not stop until you recognize your true identity. Do not stop until you are happy and free, as you deserve to be.

I have become a woman who guides others and is committed to my purpose. I am disciplined, risk-taking, and unafraid of what others say or think about me. I am more focused on using what I presently have, and I reject the "scarcity" mentality. Instead, I share all my blessings with others.

The search for perfection no longer paralyzes me. I understand that perfection can only be achieved if you master and love the process. Nothing is perfectly created the first time; we can always start with an MVP (Minimum Viable Product) and construct from there. This applies to any aspect of life.

Today I feel more fulfilled than ever. I vibrate with every step I take. I feel peace and certainty; I feel at home. If I think of all the doubts of the past, they no longer have meaning. The price of fullness can be high, but you can receive the ultimate prize: feeling fulfilled and self-realized.

I wish that you may also find your purpose so you can commit to leading a wonderful life and settle for nothing less. If you have not yet found the fullness, the spark of life, the meaning of each day and that which makes your heart vibrate every morning, keep looking because what you are looking for is also looking for you. That's why I know you'll find it.

REFLECTION QUESTIONS

1. What is the decision you have been putting off for a long time? What price are you paying for not taking that next step?

2. What area of your life should you examine and then commit to doing deep work within in order to move you to the next level?

3. How does money fit into your story? How is it influencing your decisions? What will your new story be?

BIOGRAPHY

Felissa Arias is from Santo Domingo, Dominican Republic and is the CEO and Founder of Viviendo Hablando, a personal finance consultancy. She specializes in human and professional development through the cultivation of consciousness.

Felissa has more than 20 years of experience in management and finance in the private and government sectors, including many years as budget manager for the Ministry of Foreign Affairs in Dominican Republic. After achieving professional success, she formed a high-impact community dedicated to the personal and professional growth of women that organizes programs, digital courses, webinars, and participates in financial conferences. She is interested in high-performance habits and the application of resources for the evolution of consciousness.

In 2012, Felissa received a master's degree in business management concentration strategy from the Pontificia Universidad Catolica Madre y Maestra. She has additional coursework and certifications in budgeting, planning, and public management and is fluent in Spanish, Italian, and English.

Felissa is the author of the best-seller, *Transforma tus finanzas en 30 Días: cambia tu mente, establece nuevos hábitos y logra la libertad.* She is an international speaker, creator of the program, *90 Días de Alto Rendimiento* (90DAR) and host of the podcast, *Transforma tus finanzas con Felissa.*

Felissa Arias
info@viviendohablando.com
Instagram: @viviendohablando

Lya Martinez

"Every second, we have control over our decisions."

I'm at a German train station thinking that I have to spend the night here because I have no place to sleep. This is the most enlightened place in the city in the middle of the week, where there's a lot of movement from very early in the morning until very late at night. It's a place where I can go unnoticed.

I have a feeling of emptiness in my stomach, despite having eaten very well, thanks to the restaurant owner who let me order a succulent dish from his menu in exchange for cleaning the bathrooms. "Don't worry and eat what you want to. Pay me when you have money, girl," he had told me. God bless you wherever you are at this moment!

I'm sitting on a bench with a roof, at nine o'clock in the evening in the middle of winter. I'm dressed with two pairs of socks, my somewhat wet fabric sneakers, two pants (to protect me: one put on with the closure forward and another one purposely with put on with the closure backwards), four shirts, two jackets, gloves, a scarf, and a hat. Ah! And my backpack full of personal treasures.

I am wearing the most matching, clean, and ironed clothing

possible, so I won't be mistaken for being homeless. I have a good excuse up my sleeve in case some policeman or vigilante asks me what I am doing here: "I'm travelling on the first train at dawn." The truth is I have recently arrived from Venezuela and need to get back to my friend's house where my things are so I can clean up and take a shower. Then, I can continue looking for a place to live as a new immigrant in Germany.

I fully trust that the things that happen have already been created in our minds. But what happens when I have expectations without any reason? How do I recognize that something is invented by my desire to succeed and not fail, and not from my desire to just have something tangible and realistic for me, for my life, and my happiness? How do I know what is real? How do I know that something is good and that it is best for me?

LIFE AS AN IMMIGRANT

I came to Germany to seek better health, stability, knowledge, security, love, and abundance. I knew I would be able to study, learn to see things from a different perspective, develop empathy for others and hopefully, find love. I didn't even know the language, but from the moment I first arrived in Germany, I knew immediately that I wanted to stay forever, even without being able to communicate or even say the real name of the country: Deutschland. I fell in love with it at first sight and decided to stay. However, I didn't have the resources or guidance to be able to realize that dream. That's where my true learning experience began.

Like many of us, it was difficult for me to hide. In my particular case, I didn't want to pretend I was ok, but I didn't want to worry the people who loved me since they couldn't help me, and they were also more than 7,000 kilometers away. I had to deal with the expectations of others and their criticisms and comments to me because I was a foreigner. For example, many people assumed that because I was traveling abroad, I thought I was better than everyone else, or perhaps I was a millionaire. I had to listen to their suggestions and ideas of what I should or shouldn't do, even though they didn't have the slightest idea what it was like to be an immigrant. I even heard from people I did not trust or ask for advice. I thought, HA! If they only knew. To improve my situation, I had to continuously persevere. As for being a millionaire, that wasn't such a bad idea.

Actually, by German standards, I was a newborn in a body of 28-year-old. I didn't have any information about Germany, or even know where I could take a bus. I had absolutely nothing except a suitcase with my books, my CDs, my underwear, and the desire to get ahead with constancy, perseverance, and doing everything possible to not lose my "focus."

Arriving in this new country, I found myself in the emptiness of solitude, in a place where I had no reference point. I noticed that those who were close to me did not offer any possible solutions to help me reestablish my life. On the contrary, they made me feel like I belonged nowhere. I felt like I was in "limbo" inside and out, where I had no one to hold on to but myself, my beliefs, and what I wanted at that moment.

I had mixed feelings. Despite all the sorrows, I was where I wanted to be and happy to be in Germany. It had all stemmed from my plan and desires but there were thoughts in my head and ideas that I was starting to believe: *I'm poor, I'm alone, and so far from my country.* At that moment I reflected on my life, and I was totally shocked by what I discovered.

Suddenly, something told me that I should reorganize and rethink my life because I didn't see where it was taking me. I started thinking, what do I want? What do I wish? Why did I come? Did I deserve it? What did I really feel? At what point in my life have I overcome extreme situations like this? How many times am I willing to endure living like this? What do I have to learn from this situation so that it happens as quickly as possible and I can go to the next level of the game? Will I be fine? What is the first thing I must do to get out of this situation? Thank God that at least I have my health!

That morning, that blessed morning "after the storm," the sun came out, especially for me. Sometimes we have to hit rock bottom to realize what we don't want. Many times we get lost between routine and monotony, without giving importance to the control we have or don't have over the things that happen to us. Every second, we have control over our decisions.

LEAVING THE COMFORT ZONE

Rethinking my life, leaving the circle of "desperation to survive," and entering the fluid path of "starting to live" has been one of the most important lessons of my life. It's not just about getting out of everyday situations and seeing how small things are solved on a day-to-day basis. It's about having, and in my case, not losing, my vision for my life. That is what prompted me to take the step to emigrate and live every day beyond what we now call the "comfort zone." How can one live in the "comfort zone" when you just moved from one country to another? Well, by falling into the routine of "surviving" and not simply "starting to live." In that moment of rethinking, I had to absorb my physical relocation, accept it as part of myself, and make the decision to have better moments each day to set goals and get closer to achieving them.

For me, the "comfort zone" begins when life becomes monotonous and routine. I think that sometimes people who emigrate don't change anything except their locale. They act the same way they have always acted and use their change of geography as an excuse to hide and always get the same result.

Another way to live is to have the desire for a better "quality of life" and go for it by enjoying the journey and the changes along the way. Another way is to have a life where you "do what you can" and fall into monotony almost as a self-punishment, no matter where you are. I consider that there is a very thin line between comfort and conformism. The first is a step and the second is a gap with the dangerous possibility of stagnating. Both are perfectly hidden within the routine and monotony. I think it is important to be very aware and attentive to that.

After having posed all those questions that blessed morning and answering them realistically and honestly, I made a decision to focus myself on an action plan. I would set small steps and goals with dates in the calendar to force me to achieve them in a timely manner. I would read self-help books in the public library, which is wonderful and a comfortable, warm place to go for several hours after work. Eventually, I met stable, native-born people and I was lucky to get into a gospel choir where I met Germans who are good friends today. I met my current husband as well. I also took courses at the University of Köln and although I did not complete my studies there, it was something that helped me assimilate into the culture.

Everything I did involved searching and translating or learning and translating. I devoted myself to getting to know the country where I decided to make my home. I studied its culture, its people, and tried to understand many things and never generalize. I read, read, and read, and looked for more ways to multiply my opportunities and have access to everything necessary to complete my small objectives in a harmonious way for me and for all the people involved.

FOCUSED SUCCESS

It's important to recognize the power we have within each one of us to change the direction of our path by just deciding what we honestly want for ourselves, without harming anyone along the way. At the same time, it's important to take tiny steps and achieve immediate goals without stopping. However, we should give ourselves permission to fall into drama when necessary, but only with an expiration date. We can have permission to rest, but not for too long. We must motivate ourselves again and continue with our goal so our dreams and wishes will become a reality.

Before I gained focus, nothing good happened. Once I had an action plan, everything began to improve and my horizon automatically expanded. My whole environment began to change, my life became more stable, and everything began to calm down. I met many nice people and angels began to appear in my life. I learned to use the language and its slang, without judgement and with respect. I cleansed my life of toxic people. I began to have space to experience unforgettable things. I got married and started a family. I gained a new life without losing my focus.

Now, I am lucky to have two beautiful children, be the wife of a good man, and have a beautiful, loving family that supports me. They are proud of everything I achieve every day, as I'm proud of them. I launched my own company, even in the midst of running my family and helping them get to extracurricular activities, medical appointments, etc. I go on vacations with my laptop under my arm and do my job, and I take care of myself as a person. I try to stay healthy. Nobody said that this was going to be easy, but I was always sure that it was possible.

After deciding and making a plan of action, I was able to multiply my efforts and intentions in everything, and also trust in God and in myself. And that's how I left my "comfort zone" (which had been absolutely uncomfortable) and was able to achieve my immediate objectives. I still believe workers need to work and I watch as things continue to happen, good and not so good, while I continue making decisions with focus.

REFLECTION QUESTIONS

1. Are you willing to leave your mental comfort zone?

2. Are you willing to multiply the effort to reach your life goals?

3. Are you willing to value yourself and trust in your inner strength to make decisions?

BIOGRAPHY

Lya Martinez is a proud Venezuelan wife and mother of two beautiful beings, who teach her about her self-worth every day. She comes from a neighborhood caraque, which taught her that she can change her life for the better, regardless of the opinions and situation around her. Lya is loyal, grateful, passionate about what she likes, and very detail-oriented. She has always liked uniting people under one purpose or finding something in common with someone that makes that moment something very special.

Lya graduated with a degree in programming and event management at Colegio Universitario de Caracas to achieve her dream of creating moments full of love, emotions, and exceptional detail that can count among the most memorable in our lives. This desire prompted her to launch a business which plans, organizes, and executes shows and events focused on entertainment and/or personal development with a "special touch" that is exclusive and elegant. It is called L. M. Producciones and is headquartered in Cologne, Germany. She believes that events cause great emotions and make us feel. In turn, our feelings are what identify us and define what we do with our soul.

Lya Martinez
LMProducciones@de-los-angeles.de
www.LM-Producciones.com

Andrea Villamizar López

"As long as you have yourself, nothing is missing."

Making mistakes is always a learning experience, but it is also part of the growth and evolution of change. Making changes is difficult, but the more pain, fear, and uncertainty that accompanies a change, the more important it can be.

At one time in my life, I wanted to be certain that everything that once hurt me in the depths of my being would become infinite blessings, gratitude, and teachings for the experiences that I would have to endure later. My heart broke into a thousand pieces, my company vanquished between debts, a country that was not my place of birth, a physically absent family, and a deep sense of the abyss, of loneliness, of the unknown, led me to live a limitless life that was nothing more than improvisation and a poor ability to make decisions. Those decisions cost me sleepless nights, incessant concern, physical reactions to my despair, my inability to understand what was happening, where I was going, and a myriad of questions that sooner or later found their answers.

LIFE TO BE LIVED

I remember how that illusion, the desire to live, the desire to work and create wonderful things, went out like a candle in its final stage of light. The immediate and determined solution was to cover my pain with any distraction, any person disguised as a lifeguard, anything that became a space full of nothingness, emptiness, and impossibilities. My world was transformed into a place where not even I wanted to live; my heart was sailing in the face of uncertainty and fear, and I was getting lost, faded, and uncomfortable until I forgot to enjoy the landscape, the route, the road, and the magic.

Now, I can analyze the situation with another perspective; I can look back and clearly see the lessons that pain brought me, the great morals I learned from a story existing between failure and achievement, disconnection and the path that led to finding my true self; a self that has cosme to emerge, but has given me the clarity necessary to understand who I am. I now have the drive that makes my heart beat, to feel inspired, guided, prepared and excited to live with passion every day, to contribute and help others find their own route, their destiny, the clarity of their decisions, their true selves.

As a child growing up in Venezuela, I was constantly flying in a cloud, dreaming, creating, playing characters that would take me to a wonderful place; to be a woman of the world, with an unpredictable power to deliver her message. The girl I was became a character, with certainty, and sometimes somewhat exaggerated; she was theatrical in every sense of the word. She personified the characters of my favorite series. She sang, she danced; it was clear that she wanted to be a star. Without prejudice, without fear, without expectations, she loved to see the eyes of people enjoying her interpretations, amazed at the naïveté and fearlessness of such a young girl. That girl was absolutely certain of what she wanted for herself later in life, and never wondered how she would get there because dreaming was allowed. After all, who cared about the "how" if she was very clear about the what.

Oh, how I wish this sense of security accompanied me during the rest of my adolescence and adulthood, but unfortunately it wasn't so; the older I grew, the more insecure and detached from my purpose I became.

I was always a very protected, well-cared for girl, perhaps because at that time, my food choices were a constant struggle. I had to learn to nourish myself beyond the sweets I loved and in which I found my refuge. As I grew and matured, the protection of my parents continued to exist, but now it was up to me to make my own plan, my own decisions, and finally, leave the nest, where I would grow even more. There, I could be more understanding and guided by my own intuition and my desire to have that life I dreamed about, and my ability to make it come true.

My ability to communicate ideas became increasingly evident, and my way of connecting with other people became my most precious treasure. It led me to study journalism; a career that would give structure to what I did spontaneously, naturally, something that was tattooed in my veins. Today, more than ever, I understand my potential as a journalist, but from a different angle, a different approach.

COLOMBIA

After years of exercising my career, being an entrepreneur in my country, almost without warning, almost without analyzing it and driven by a situation that I couldn't control, it was time to leave. I was married to a wonderful man who gave me great experiences, great moments by his side, whom I love and for whom I still have very deep feeling. I'm thankful for what it meant in my life; a deep love, complicity, friendship, adventure and dreams, with whom I had great projects and to whom I owe much of what I am now. For about eight months, I committed myself to that love. I was married by the court, through the church, and I broke with tradition and a beautiful friendship (which I recovered later). I left home with my new husband and moved out of the country. It may sound simple, but the sum of all these events began to open a wound that years later would begin to hurt, bleed, and require my maximum attention.

I arrived in the city of Medellín in Columbia full of deep nostalgia for having left the known, for abandoning that sense of security that transmitted through me when I was close to my parents, my brothers, my nephews, my family. Today, I sincerely believe that I wasn't prepared for so many changes, so soon, so often; that little girl became an adult in a very short period of time. All too soon, she had to spread her wings and fly far from the usual, from the known, from the everyday. My move to a new city was the beginning of my master's degree, to work for others when I'd been working for my own dreams for more than seven years. I had always dreamed of being a wife and living as a responsible adult.

After a while, I met a woman who helped me. We had met in the fashion world and everyone told me it was the most profitable business in that city. I bet on the idea of having my own clothing brand. After two years, I found myself opening my first business as a foreigner.

I began to create the brand, to structure what I wanted it to be and to work for it. Without a doubt, the decision to set up my fashion business was created by the comments of those around me who agreed that it was a good way to start building a life from scratch in another country.

My sponsor was a woman who loved fashion but had no idea about the world or running a business. I consulted with professional people in that area and the project became a reality; a beautiful reality that came to have very satisfactory achievements in a short period of time. However, I was convinced that I was doing it for the business itself. There was no passion, nor excessive love that would keep me sailing in the sea of calm waters or even storms for a long time. Recognizing this reality, my body constantly suffered from excessive fear, reacted to any impulse in an alarming and somewhat exaggerated way, between panic attacks, lack of sleep, hypochondria, and more. I began my journey to doctors, specialists, religions, or any help that would allow me to understand what was happening in me.

I was really married to the man of my dreams, I had a business that supported me, I was safe in another country and my family, although they were far away, were supportive. My increasingly deteriorating physical health led me to begin the journey towards the questions that needed answers.

After being medicated for obsessive compulsive disorder, I reached an endocrine doctor who diagnosed me with an autoimmune disease that attacks the thyroid, known as Graves' Disease. Beginning with excisions of radioactive iodine, life was a relentless adventure to regain control of my body. I felt completely lost, strange in my own skin. It was like residing in a reality that didn't belong to me. This was so far from that girl who perfectly understood how she wanted to lead her story.

Every day I felt more locked up, a prisoner of circumstance, of the unknown and increasingly scared. That great love became the victim of my pain, my fears, my deepest sufferings, my mistakes, and my bad decisions. The low point of our marriage eventually arrived, and with it, the decision to let it go, to let me go.

I needed to find myself. I needed to be able to look at myself in the mirror and be certain of who I was, calmly, peacefully, and safely, without causing so much pain in the face of my own instability that I dragged down and destroyed everything I touched. At that moment, my ability to concentrate, to continue building a business, was completely null. Being such an emotional and sensitive person, my broken heart left me without a desire to continue. I could no longer continue rowing; I gave up, and in that surrender, I found myself vulnerable, alone, and missing myself. That silence would take over every pore of my being until my soul gave me the necessary answers to find my way back home, to find myself.

BACK TO ME

Long story short, I suffered the pain of collapsing fortresses that had protected my essence for so many years. I began to undress entirely, to spend long nights awake, drowned in tears, looking for answers. Self-help books became my hobby, my allies. Friends were where I found shelter; I openly began to ask everyone who knew me what they thought of me, and what escape they saw for me in this dark moment of my life. How could I recover from a divorce, a bankruptcy of a company, endless debts, and how could I start over? In their own way, they gave me ideas; they reminded me of what a great listener I was, that I could write, communicate, understand, and help others.

I think that it was just at that moment that the transition began which up until today has become my greatest and deepest purpose and my hope for the future. Always (and I say always because this happened to me), in those moments of life, people appear who become lights along the road, undeniable companions who mark a great trajectory at each step, people who leave traces and who trust in you and give you opportunities until they see you succeed.

That's how thanks to a man that I call "my angel," I came to Spain, to try to repair the pieces, to find my way again, to discover myself far from everything, but closer to my being. I began the most rewarding journey, full of joy and satisfaction towards the discovery of my passion. Journalism, with personal development, became the tool that allowed me to meet and forgive myself. I wanted my story to become a sufficient reason to help others and here, almost three years later, I find again the pleasant idea that so much raw pain would become my greatest legacy.

Allow those internal questions to have answers that come from your own wisdom. Every decision is certain when it comes from you, and remember that there's no darkness, loneliness, or sadness if you have, if you know, if you give yourself deep, unconditional love, full of trust and dedication. I'm still sure that as long as you have yourself, nothing is missing.

REFLECTION QUESTIONS

1. How are you now the same and how are you different from when you were younger? Why?

2. In moments of greatest vulnerability, where do you find your shelter?

3. What change in your life has given you the greatest understanding of yourself?

BIOGRAPHY

Andrea Villamizar López is a woman who seeks the clarity of knowledge and the landscape to understand who she is and where she is going. She is a relentless seeker of passions and purposeful lives.

As a child in Maracaibo, Venezuela, she developed the ability to transform ideas and thoughts into projects. She trained as a social communicator in broadcast journalism, which allowed her to use her interviewing skills to open people's minds and invite them into personal reflection.

Andrea is currently a professional coach and emotional Intelligence trainer in neurolinguistic programming, certified by D'Arte Human & Business School and Meta International. The program's most ambitious goal is for every human being to trust, believe in, and understand what they bring to this world. She dreams of helping people become motivated, happy, inspired, and full of desire to continue on this journey of life with more resources and a deeper self-knowledge of what moves their world. Andrea seeks love in everything she touches - the love that moves masses and the love that is available to everyone.

Andrea Villamizar López
andrea@veoyvivo.com
+34 645402125

Andrea Mesis-Bruno

"It's ok to be present over perfect."

When I was 19, I knew exactly what I wanted to become. Sort of. I wanted to make $100,000 a year, drive a BMW, and vice president of something by the time I was 30. Does that sound like a driven overachiever? That's what I was!

I can attribute some of this ambition to my mother, who was my ultimate inspiration. In fact, we had a friendly competition between us for the title of most successful "boss lady" in the family.

IN HER SHOES

Mom came to the U.S. from Jamaica when she was only nine years old. She met my Cuban father in New Jersey before joining the Navy right after graduating high school and being deployed to Okinawa where she was stationed. Unfortunately, dad was stationed in South America, so they had to get married when they were both on leave. Mom became pregnant with my older sister on her honeymoon, and when she started to show, she returned to the U.S. and waited for my father to return.

At first, she was a stay-at-home mom like most women of

her day, raising her daughters in a Manhattan suburb. But when her marriage began to sour, she became a single parent and stepped into her high heels. Literally. I remember them because my mom's shoes were the finishing touch on her professional attire as she headed out the door to her job in customer service at a pharmaceutical company. I loved those shoes and borrowed whenever she'd let me steal them!

My mom was larger than life, a true "boss lady" and the take-charge type who would say anything to anybody. Her body was adorned with tattoos and I would lovingly tease her that they were all total clichés. She made single motherhood look easy. We always had everything we needed, and she was a rock I could depend on. I took it for granted that she would always be there for me.

Then, in her fifties, my mother was diagnosed with lung cancer and had one of her lungs removed. She never smoked, and the only reason we could find to explain her cancer was her work at the pharmaceutical company or her time in the Navy. I took my mother into my home while she received treatment at Memorial Sloan Kettering. Her illness was a wake-up call and turning point. It forced me to take a good hard look at my life, where I was, where I was going, and where I wanted to be.

SECURITY CHECK

Professionally, I have always stuck out as a sore thumb as one of the few women (and Latinas no less!) employed in security. I loved it. Driving from my home in New Jersey to the hustling, bustling Big Apple very day made me feel like an industry trailblazer. I believe security is a great industry for women that can be very lucrative too. It's a respectable alternative to law enforcement, which was once my original goal, and a good option for women who are looking for a career off the well- worn, stereotypical "female" path of teacher or administrator.

However, security people are on call all the time, even when they are not officially on call. When shootings or terrorist attacks happened anywhere, we needed to ramp up the security at our client's facilities. As a quasi-first responder, I would be on hand for additional security manpower, information dispatch, and creating a calming environment for their tenants.

On 9/11, I was driving into Manhattan when the planes struck the World Trade Center (WTC). After making sure my own family was secure, I immediately reported to a disaster recovery site, which was the SunGuard NOC (Network Operations Center), to secure it during all the chaos in the financial district.

The next day, we worked tirelessly to prepare for the professional refugees who had escaped from the WTC. They were heaped in despair and occasionally burst into tears for those who may or may not have survived. We were responsible for ensuring their safety and comfort, alongside grief counselors, law enforcement, and security personnel, still semi-dazed themselves but holding it together for the people in full-blown crisis. SunGuard set about constructing a temporary trading floor to resume the commodities exchange and our company provided the security needed to reboot the critical trading communication line that was lost in the rubble. I'll never forget the dramatic tension a week later when, with fingers crossed, they flipped the switch to the newly restored data connection to open trading again. For the next few weeks, I was working almost 24 hours a day, seven days a week, to secure facilities and make people feel safe again. It was our job, but our patriotic duty as well.

Until my mom got sick, I hadn't thought about how I had not yet achieved my 19-year-old plan. Now, as I watched her body ravaged, I knew I needed to begin moving intentionally towards my life goals. I needed to create the life I had always wanted.

Even after Mom beat her cancer, I still ignored my plans and wasn't moving forward. To the outside world, my life was perfect. I emulated my mother, doing everything for everyone and never missing a beat. I had a beautiful house, a wonderful family, and breezily hosted every party. I was the one dropping off my son, picking up the dry cleaning, and heading home to make dinner. I did it all and probably made it look easy, just like Mom did. I wanted to achieve the perfect marriage too, like my grandparents, who in their seventies were still very flirty and affectionate with each other.

In reality, though, I wasn't being present in my own life. I was too busy being busy to see it. When I finally reflected on my marriage, I came to some conclusions. For a marriage to work, spouses must understand each other's needs. The 24-hour on-call, the long hours, and other matters of our relationship were eroding our marriage. We became what neither of us wanted. In 2014, my husband and I decided to divorce and settled upon joint custody of our son, DJ, who is the love of my life and my everything.

Luckily, I was growing my skills and learning to say "yes" at work. I had been managing a large portfolio of uniformed security officers when, in 2015, I was asked to take over the security technology division that at the time, was a small team of two. We then acquired a larger company, which promoted me to department head supervising 20 security specialists. It was a daunting challenge, but I said "yes" and eventually figured it all out. By embracing responsibilities and opportunities that came my way, I became a badass "boss lady" in my own right, which made my mother proud.

Sadly in 2017, she died on my birthday, not of cancer but of a pulmonary aneurism at the age of 59. My heart was ripped from me. How could I adjust to life as a single mother without the support and encouragement of the most amazing role model of single motherhood?

Now I was really on my own, without my mom or a husband to rely on. I had thought divorce would be great, with lots of freedom and a chance to explore myself, but I found it quite the opposite. I necessarily began to become more present in my life, experiencing it all more viscerally, but not always positively. While grieving two big losses, I beheld my mother's cherished shoe collection, now mine, and I selected a pair and dove into work, sure that she would approve. I wouldn't be perfect, but it was ok to be present over perfect. I began carrying out my 19-year-old plan, dedicating each triumph to my mother's memory.

CITY ESCAPE

After the divorce, I had promised DJ that I would make up for everything and provide all he needed to experience life to the fullest. I moved to a national company that I thought would give me the stability that I longed for, but I found I was more satisfied working for a smaller, local company that better understood the market. I started sending the universe signals I wanted more, and that's when life got amazing.

During my career, I got to know many professionals who expertly navigated the exciting, magical world of Manhattan real estate. I was recruited by Enobrac Plumbing, which specializes in some of the largest core and shell plumbing and sprinkling development projects in New York. Many people ask me about the name Enobrac. I'll tell you the secret. If you read the name of the company backwards, you will see the name of the company's founder and quite a character in the industry!

Today I gratefully contribute to a fast-paced, dynamic, multi-billion-dollar Manhattan real estate market with the energetic tenacity of our "reverse namesake." Sound like fun? It is! It's a magical world where negotiating deals sometimes has more to do with your reputation and your client relationships than anything else. Some days are like the Shark Tank television show and others involve deep research on the personal attributes of the client to earn their trust. It doesn't hurt to support their charitable causes or find out what's most important to them and why.

Best of all, thanks to this new career I have been able to

check off some of the boxes in my 19-year-old plan. Ok, I'm a little over 30 years old but I have finally achieved the title of vice president of client relations at Enobrac. My salary has escalated, and I didn't get the BMW but I did have a pretty sweet Mercedes! Best of all, I have been able to keep my promise to DJ.

Everyone who knows me knows DJ. I always say he's the best of his parents: sensitive like me, and confident like his dad. He's grown into a compassionate, caring and supportive young man. He's part of my life, whatever I'm doing, and he has been able to share in my success in wonderful ways. We've gone on amazing vacations and he's been at my side as I popped the cork of my mom's favorite champagne, Moet Ice Imperial, when celebrating our new home. He's been able to meet his heroes like goalie Luis Robles of the New York Red Bulls. He's practiced at Citi Field with the all-time legends of the Mets as I negotiated a construction deal. He's watched the New York Nets and Knicks play from luxury suites, golfed along the shores of Puerto Rico, and enjoyed countless other special moments. He understands what I do, the hours I keep, and he is proud of me as I am of him.

We recently moved into a brand new house and it's wonderful to think it has all happened from pursuing that plan I made so long ago. He's going to attend one of the best STEM high schools in the country so that his dreams may come true, too. Everything has come full circle.

I've also tried to give DJ an example of community service and philanthropy. I assist Caring to Remember for Alzheimer's Research, Tuesday's Children, an organization that supports the children of the fallen (9/11 as well as military), and Maestro Cares, an organization which improves the quality of life for orphaned children throughout Latin America. DJ and I have personally travelled to the Maestro Cares orphanage in Ponce, Puerto Rico to witness the impact of their hard work and generosity.

Working in security, then watching my mother survive cancer only to be suddenly torn from my world, I am keenly aware that anything can happen at any time. When it does, it's nice to know I have people I love to support me. It's also nice to know I can always be the boss lady of my own life, just like mom was.

REFLECTION QUESTIONS

1. Did you make goals for yourself when you were younger? What are you doing to reach them?

2. Can you think of a time you said "yes" to an opportunity that made you nervous?

3. Besides your employer, who do you work for?

BIOGRAPHY

Andrea Mesis-Bruno has a long career of succeeding in roles typically held by men. After more than twenty years in commercial security, she is now Vice President for Enobrac Plumbing and works with the most demanding developers in NYC to sculpt the city's ever-changing skyline.

She is a champion for young women pursuing the trades and other non-traditional roles and has mastered the delicate balance of being a loving single mom and powerful construction executive. Andrea takes part in countless charities lending her influence to raise valuable funds including Tuesday's Children, Caring to Remember, and Maestro Cares. In 2006 she served as the Young Professional Liaison for the American Society of Industrial Security and assisted college graduates in finding a career path in private law enforcement and security technology. Andrea also started a mentorship program for NEW (Nontraditional Employment for Women) to assist women in developing a career path after completing construction development projects in NYC.

Andrea is raising her son, DJ, who is her inspiration and motivation for her hard work. Together they have traveled together to the Maestro Cares orphanage in Ponce, Puerto Rico in 2019 and live each day with a sense of gratitude and a desire to make a difference.

Andrea Mesis-Bruno
andreamesisbruno@enobrac.com
646.210.8343

Denise Pedroza Sandoval

"There are three things in life no one can take away from you: your happiness, your experiences, and your identity."

It is important to remember where we come from so that we can appreciate where we want to go. I would not be the person I am today without the foundation my parents gave me. I will eternally be grateful to them for making the brave choice to leave their roots behind to create a new life in the U.S. I know they faced many challenges along the way so I wouldn't have to struggle.

My childhood, as I recall it, was a happy one. I grew up with four siblings in Cicero, Illinois. We cleaned our home listening to Juan Gabriel. When I completed my chores, I was rewarded with PAL gum. *Nana & Tata's* (grandma and grandpa's) home was where I indulged in Oreo cookies and played with my cousins. We had huge family gatherings where we played poker, Mexican games like *Loteria* and *Pirinola*, and had pizza nights. I also grew up eating the best turkey and enchiladas *potosinas* ever. I was a petite girl filled with hopes and dreams.

On May 20, 2000 at the age of 13, I wrote a letter to myself about my dreams. One dream was to visit Paris, but it was the ending of the letter that stayed with me. Before signing my name, I wrote "Promise to study hard. Hard work pays off. Look back and laugh." I signed it: D.S. Little did I know that many life experiences awaited me and would shape me into who I am today; and they were completely different than what my 13-year-old self had in mind!

HAPPINESS IS A CHOICE

Initially, I believed I was the author of my own destiny. Although I still believe that, it is also true that life gave me many unexpected events that helped me grow. Some events were positive, others were negative. These unexpected events altered my story, but I kept pushing towards my happy ending. I questioned what happiness meant for me, but I was over-thinking it. By overcoming challenges and accepting my faith, I began to recognize that my happiness came from simple things in life: living a peaceful life, seeing my family healthy, dancing, and spending quality time with those I love. Today I understand that in order for me to completely recognize the true meaning of happiness, I have to first live through experiences that make me feel joyful, betrayed, vulnerable, powerless, fearless, grateful, different, discouraged, misunderstood, judged, hopeful, empowered, stressed, and accomplished.

I found my happiness in my studies, living my life based on my expectations, and traveling the world with my best friend, my now husband, D.P. I decided to live my life with intention, prioritize my self-care and do things I enjoy. I chose a career that fulfills me, and I married the man my heart chose and began to create beautiful memories that I will be able to take with me wherever I go. I made the choice to be happy, because in the end, choosing to be happy was and is my responsibility.

LESSONS FROM EXPERIENCE

Diverse life experiences not only mark us but strengthen us too. I learned to accept the pain from negative experiences, but never forget the important lessons. Here is a glimpse of my life experiences that shaped who I am.

During my junior high years, I was chosen to be a peer mediator for my school. I helped other students solve relationship problems. This positive experience inspired me to develop an interest in working with people. The skills I used to help others as a teen served me as an adult, since my brain is now wired to focus on solutions, rather than problems.

As time passed, I also had painful experiences that not only taught me important life lessons but also caused me physical and emotional wounds. Even girls who have a plan to thrive experience emotional crisis along the way. I know I did. At the age of 16, I learned that impulsive acts can lead to serious consequences.

In an attempt to run away from home, I had an accident where I fell, hurt my back, and was temporarily confined to a wheelchair. With the support of my mother, family, loyal friends, and an awesome physical therapist, I regained movement of my legs. Today, I dance like no one is watching. The experience was a defining moment for me where I learned to forgive and recognize that no matter how many times I fell, I had to keep trying.

The betrayal of a high school friend taught me the importance of being loyal. I am beyond grateful for my circle of best friends today; you all know who you are.

During my time at Morton East High School, it was my English and my Algebra teachers who taught me the valuable lesson of believing in myself. Whenever I doubted my math and writing skills, it was they who gave me words of encouragement. "Be more confident in your answers, Denise; one day you will do great things," they said. Mr. Antus and Ms. Kane, thank you for believing in me when I didn't. Madame Jenks homeschooled me for my French classes when I couldn't attend school due to my injury. Madame Jenks, thank you for not giving up on me.

The stereotype of growing up in Cicero with limited opportunities for success only motivated me to work harder. The Mexican cultural expectation that a girl has to know how to cook before marriage, marry at an early age, *antes que se te pase el tren* (before the train passes by), pushed me to create a different identity from the typical Mexican woman, known only for cooking and cleaning. I wanted to create an identity for myself apart from cultural expectations, and most importantly, one based on my needs and my own values.

In the summer of 2004, I moved into my dorm at Southern Illinois University. The minute my parents left, I felt a profound sadness. I realized being six hours away from home for a psychology program was probably not a good idea. It was in that instant that I understood the phrase, "You do not know what you have until it's gone." They weren't even gone five minutes and I was already missing them. I cried, but all I could do was prove to myself I could handle it. I had a promise to fulfill.

When I ended a summer relationship, I learned the term "breakup violence." My relationship with this man had never been violent, but when I decided to break up with him, he decided to bite me. Since the incident occurred at school, I was escorted from school premises and suspended for disturbing the peace, even though I was the one attacked. My self-esteem was damaged, my sense of security was shaken, and my education was paused. Through this traumatic experience, I learned the true meaning of being stalked, how to obtain an order of protection, how to report a stolen vehicle, and how the legal system failed me when I needed it most. The nightmare taught me to be more aware, fearless, and beyond grateful that my life did not end on a later night when he used his vehicle as a weapon to try to hurt me. The physical scar he left on me is the only thing remaining from that negative experience. I refused to give him further power over me. I wasn't a victim; I was a victor because in the end, he didn't defeat me.

I transferred to a different school for the rest of my undergraduate years, and when I looked around, I quickly noticed my classmates did not sound like or look like me. I felt out of place. However, I didn't let this feeling hold me back. Whether or not I felt out of place, I knew I belonged there and had a promise to keep.

I was optimistic that life would offer me positive experiences, and it was just a matter of time. I began my healing process by volunteering at the PADS suburban shelter at St. Mary of Celle in Berwyn. I also volunteered as an usher, catechist, and served as the twelve o'clock mass coordinator at Good Shepherd Church in Chicago.

I overcame the challenges by accepting the lessons and confronting one situation at a time. I also grew closer to church. Finally, the unexpected and lovely time arrived when life decided to cross my path with D.P. It was the right time, place, and happened in the best way possible, Salsa dancing.

D.P. came into my life and was there for me when I felt the world was unsafe. He made me feel hopeful again. I had the desire to be me again and I was determined to one day look back and laugh at everything. He understood my way of viewing life and he was smart, a great dancer, and had values similar to mine. In 2011, I married the love of my life, Daniel Pedroza.

Then there are those experiences you would never wish upon anyone. A year after my wedding, my mother was hospitalized and had an operation. Suddenly, all my dreams simply did not matter; it was then I instantly learned that there are things in life that money can't buy. Fortunately, my mother is healthy today, and I learned that doctors can also misdiagnose.

As an adult, I experienced the real world. I worked a morning shift, attended my internship in the afternoon, and went to graduate school at night. During my master-level internship, I experienced discrimination from my supervisor. It was this experience that taught me to be assertive. If I didn't speak my mind and verbalize my needs and dislikes, who would do it for me?

I studied my DSM-V (Diagnostic Statistical Manual of Mental Health Disorders) during my rides on the train. Winters were horrible and trust me when I say Chicago earned its nickname as the Windy City. I did it all while juggling to maintain a household. I doubted myself. Yet, it was this specific adult experience that taught me the meaning of perseverance. One day, our savings account had only fifty dollars in it. This forced me to quickly learn the concept of needs versus wants. I was committed to the chaos and in the end, this proud Mexican-American girl from Cicero, who promised herself at age 13 to study hard, walked that stage and graduated with her master's degree.

REINVENT YOUR IDENTITY

Don't let the difficult times define who you are. As human beings, we all can learn to accept what you have control over and let go of what you don't. For those who have suffered, don't get caught up in the past. The time and energy you invest will not change it. Instead, invest that energy to heal, forgive, ask for forgiveness, and create changes in your life. Discover what makes you happy and reinvent your identity if necessary. Let your experiences inspire you to keep going. Create new memories; it's never too late.

We all have a past, and we all have the ability to change.

Don't compare your life to others; instead take control of your story and find your happy ending. If you are wondering if I ever got to Paris, I'm happy to report that I did, and on more than one occasion, with people I love.

As I look back, I can now laugh and realize that my story was meant to be this way. There are three things in life which nobody can take away from you: your happiness, your experiences, and your identity. The promise continues, and as a certain 13-year-old once said, hard work pays off.

I dedicate this chapter to my parents, all my family, my dear husband, amazing friends, to my lovely M.A.M., angels above, and to all those who have endured pain.

REFLECTION QUESTIONS

1. What makes you genuinely happy? What steps are you taking to be happy?

2. What have you learned about your life experiences? What did you take from the positive ones? What did you take from the negative ones?

3. 3. What new identity do you want to create yourself? What steps will you begin to take to get where you want to be?

BIOGRAPHY

Denise Pedroza Sandoval is the owner of Denise Pedroza Sandoval, LCPC, LLC. She is a Licensed Clinical Professional Counselor (LCPC) in Illinois. She obtained a bachelor of science degree in psychology from Loyola University Chicago and a master of education degree in community counseling from DePaul University. Denise is a certified PREPARE/ENRICH facilitator, providing couples therapy. She is a certified anger management specialist by the National Anger Management Association (NAMA). Denise is also trained in EMDR (Eye Movement Desensitization and Reprocessing).

Throughout her career, Denise has worked as a bilingual psychotherapist in diverse settings such as Catholic Charities, Heartland Alliance, and Pillars Community Health. She also served as an ambassador for the Young Professional Advisory Board for *Mujeres Latinas en Acción* and chair for the Community Development Committee. Denise actively participates in community events and shares her knowledge to build a more trauma-informed community.

With almost a decade in the mental health field, Denise works to increase awareness of the importance of prioritizing mental health and reducing the stigma behind it in the Latino Community. She is currently working on growing her private practice, publishing a book on breakup violence, writing children's mental health books, and traveling the world.

Denise Pedroza Sandoval
Denise@pedrozasandovaltherapy.com
(708) 955-1522

Mylene Fernström

"We remember "Excellent" people for their results."

Have you ever wondered what the key to success and the turning point for great people and companies is? The answer is "Excellence!"

Have you ever thought that you could treat your life as a masterpiece? Have you ever wondered how? Well, the answer is also "Excellence!"

Excellence is one of the most powerful differentiators in the world. For me, Excellence is poetry! For me Excellence is magic! Excellence is that little big thing that makes the difference between the mediocre and the extraordinary.

But first, we need to understand that "Excellence is not perfection; Excellence is progress." "Excellence is not an act; Excellence is a habit." "To be Excellent, you have to be obsessed with continuous improvement." "Excellence means taking care of all the details" and "Excellence means running the extra mile."

Excellence, on one hand, implies being humble and taking responsibility. It's accepting what we are and where we are. On the other hand, Excellence implies ambition, greatness, discipline, and strength to keep us pulling out of where we are up to a higher place, accepting and welcoming change. So, let's start to use the keys of being Excellent to make our life and our business extraordinary masterpieces.

THE WHAT AND HOW OF EXCELLENCE

People used to ask me, "What do I get from Excellence? Why is it important to be Excellent?"

When you pursue Excellence, your life will be surrounded by small victories that will lead to big ones, and your self-confidence will increase. You will become a stronger person and a role model for yourself and for others, such as your children, your spouse, your parents, your boss, your employees, your community, and even the world. The impact of Excellence goes in all directions, including back to you. Excellence implies a holistic view, as it is needed in all areas, to achieve the Excellent balance.

Excellence will be the greatest source of your greatness. You achieve success. You become memorable and different from many others. You become an expert on what you do and you stop wasting time in life and become a master at time management and in your life. In business you will get more sales and profitability. You will get in touch with your own happiness and growth. And most importantly, you will leave a legacy.

But to activate Excellence, you have to deactivate bad habits and instead work constantly on the good habits. As I always say, Excellence is not what stresses you; what stresses you are the bad habits, the wasted time, the lack of focus, the lack of results, the activities that don't give anything in return or lead you away from your long-term goal. These bad habits only keep us busy on the level of mediocrity.

Perfectionism, for instance, is one of those bad habits that we need to deactivate. Never look for perfection. You will get exhausted and disappointed, and the only one who is perfect is God. Instead, we can be Excellent. After all, God created us to co-create our lives with Excellence.

Perfectionism tends to make us continue with tasks forever. When perfectionism is leading us, we never feel we are ready, or good enough. That's why, many times, we get stressed and sick.

My proposal is: "Be Excellent by ending where you start, concluding and delivering what you promise on time, and adding one "cherry on top" to it. Excellence is that "cherry on top" when you create moments in life or when you deliver a product or a service that will elevate the experience every single time on everything." Perfection is short term. Excellence is long term.

To be Excellent, we have to start by getting used to doing small things extraordinarily well. Don't wait until the big things appear to do them extraordinarily. This is the best way to make Excellence a habit, not a single act. Excellence has to be applied to all the things we do. Be a master of good habits, not a victim of bad ones.

By replacing the bad habits with good habits, you will get more impact. An easy first step is to start the day by making the bed every morning, leaving it impeccable. This is the first achievement of the day, your first victory, your first drop of joy for your spirit. Transform your bedroom into a hotel room – beautiful, clean, tidy, and usable, of course.

People say that it takes time to create a masterpiece. I would say if you commit to Excellence, then the process will take less time than it normally would. On the other hand, the mark you leave will be stronger. It means that with Excellence, we are in charge of making our own lives into masterpieces. Persistence is the key and you have to act as a master.

ATTITUDE OF EXCELLENCE

There is no perfect life, but we can have a greater attitude towards life. Life is not easy, but can be simple. Focus on your most important activity and finalize it. What do you want for your life? Maybe a peaceful life? Maybe a house in the mountains? Maybe lots of time with your loved ones? Maybe a luxurious life? Maybe you want to travel around the world? Anything you want is fine! Everybody is different. Start over. It doesn't matter if you have done it already. Remember that nowadays, people live longer lives, so it's never too late. Never give up! To make your life your own masterpiece requires courage in many ways: the courage to honor you, the courage to honor your emotions, the courage to honor your deepest desires and the courage to honor your dreams.

In the pursuit of Excellence, you know that fear and failure will come, but you can confront them with a learner's attitude and see them as opportunities and lessons learned. Everything is about your attitude. Never take a victim's position or attitude. Instead, an Excellent mind identifies, creates, and takes opportunities from fear and failure. An Excellent mind has an attitude of continuous improvement.

So what is the secret to being Excellent? Excellence requires positive leadership that creates an impact. Excellence requires an obsession to keep the focus, discipline, and persistence needed to be your own leader and to design your own life or design your own company. You have to have a winner mentality to compete against yourself, to compete against your own standards, and become better, be number one, be the first. You don't compare or envy, because you know you have your own strengths, and you know your own value.

How many times have you been proud of something you have created or something you have done? Have you ever thought about how the greatest people we admire have created masterpieces, leaving their legacy and heritage for generations? Similarly, have you ever thought about how the greatest companies have created products or services that we will never forget because they transformed lives or have had an important impact on an industry or in the world? Well, these are their masterpieces. These are companies of Excellence. These are peak performers. They are all Excellent.

Excellence is putting your life in high gear. An Excellent individual, an Excellent company and Excellent leader do their best even when they are at their lowest point. If you are going to care about what others think about you, then always do things extraordinarily.

Be a leader! Believe it or not, you are always an inspiration to others. Smile even when you are tired or worried. Besides, by smiling and laughing, even if you don't feel like it, you activate and release positive hormones like oxytocin, which at the same time is the root of creativity and problem solving! You get the solution to your problem, and now you can smile and laugh for real!

As Oprah Winfrey says, "Good luck is when preparation meets opportunity." I think what happens in reality is that when you have prepared yourself well enough, opportunity will find you. Preparation in this case means practice, practice, practice. Preparation means action. Preparation doesn't mean studying forever because we believe we are not ready yet. You can only become a master when you try more times than the average person did. This is the way the best athletes take themselves to the top-- by training more hours than others. And when they are at the top, they train more. My recommendation is to practice business, practice sales!

My father always said to me, "The pupil has to become better than the master." The pupil looks, learns, and implements, but after a certain time of being exposed to different situations and scenarios from those the master knows, the pupil gets new tools and becomes even more accomplished than the master.

LIVING THE EXCELLENT LIFE

We remember Excellent people for their results. We remember masterpieces for their impact. So, what do you need to prioritize and do in order to achieve the most important result? And more specifically, what is that single activity that is critical to complete before any other? Maybe people are watching us, but must importantly, are you watching you? So let's stop thinking that no one cares about what you do because you care about what you do, and you should do it! Keep doing everything so extraordinarily well that people will come to you with offers. In the end, what counts is your results, and results don't lie.

Excellence and masterpieces come from a place of pure LOVE and are distributed to the world from a genuine place of GIVING. Kindness is what always leaves a mark and will make you memorable. Always keep a mix of compassion and leadership in your life.

Being a Colombian who moved to Sweden because I always wanted an international life, I have always seen myself as an ambassador and role model. After all, people regard you as a representative of the people from your home country. Early on, I understood my own strengths as well as Colombia's. Nowadays, I am Swedish as well, which means I am an ambassador and a role model for Sweden too. It's a great responsibility, without a doubt, but I enjoy it. I am obsessed about adding value to my work, to people, and to myself. I enjoy adding the world's perspective. Adding value for me means putting the "cherry on top," making life moments extraordinary with my mission to transmit the knowledge on Excellence to all, and to take care of Excellence in my own life.

The best news is that a superpower lies inside all of us. So let's start to treat our life as a masterpiece through the long-term power of Excellence.

REFLECTION QUESTIONS

1. What are you doing to treat your life as a masterpiece?

2. What are some examples of how you put the "cherry on top" at work and with family?

3. Who looks to you as a role model towards Excellence? Are you a good one?

BIOGRAPHY

Mylene Fernström is a multiple Excellence Award winner, creator of the concept of "Excellence Management," founder of the company www.excellencemanagement.com and author of *"The Book on Excellence-How to Become Memorable and Build Cultures of Self-Excellence,"* also available in Spanish. Mylene is an international speaker, mentor, and Excellence strategist.

Mylene is a chemical engineer and e-Commerce Manager from Colombia whose pursuit for Excellence led her to study as an exchange student in Sweden in 1990. She has lived there ever since.

At 19 years old, Mylene finished her engineering studies, and made the decision to work only with companies who were the best in their fields and committed to excellence. She has 25 years of professional achievements working in multinational companies such as 3M, Volvo Cars, Aker Kvaerner and Metso Power. In 1996, she received the Excellence Award in Volvo Cars in Sweden and in 2017, she won the Authors Award in London, UK.

Mylene's mission is to contribute to a world of Excellence by teaching others how to manage their Self-Excellence, which characterizes all great people and high-level businesses. She is convinced that bringing excellent people together is necessary to build families, businesses and countries of Excellence.

Mylene Fernström
mylene@excellencemanagement.com
Instagram: excellence_top1

THE POWER TO MANIFEST

Marielys Ávila

*"Everything we do is done from the energy that connects us and
allows us to co-create with the universe."*

I first learned about the energy of the universe from my
grandmother. When I was five years old, growing up in Caracas,
Venezuela, she would talk to me about "speaking to the universe"
and "being one with the universe." I thought about that for
a while. I had never heard the universe speak before, but my
grandma said she was in conversation with it all the time. Finally,
I concluded that she must have relationships with aliens on other
planets and in constant communication with them! Surely that's
what she meant when she spoke about talking to the universe.

Needless to say, it took a while to grow to a point where
I knew what she was talking about. Now that I do, I'm a full
believer in the power of the universe and it's my mission in life to
help others understand and believe in it too.

EUROPEAN DREAM

I was my mother's only child, and my grandmother and
I were very close. When I was 12, she gave me a book called, *I
Give You Everything That You Want*. It focused on manifesting

your dreams through the power of the universe. Back then, we called Europe "the old continent," and I had a dream to go there. "Nobody in our family has ever gone to Europe," my grandmother said when I told her my dream. "It would be very difficult for a girl from a poor country to go to Europe." Then she finished hopefully, "But you can go if you really want to." It was one of the first big dreams I sent to the universe to help manifest.

Then, when I was 19 years old, I met the man of my dreams, literally, in a disco one weekend. He was Dutch and on vacation in Caracas. We hit it off immediately and began a whirlwind courtship.

My parents were not so excited. They didn't like the foreigner who was interested in their daughter and they were very concerned that he was ten years older. As we grew closer, we knew we wanted to be together, and because he owned his own company, it made more sense for me to move to the Netherlands than for him to move to Venezuela. I had visited him a few times by then and realized that it was the next logical step.

My family didn't think so though. They were concerned that we were going to live together without getting married, but in the Dutch culture, most people didn't marry and spirituality was not a big part of their society. After I made the final move to be with him, my father did not speak to me for a year.

The move was a real culture shock for me! I didn't appreciate the chilly, gray weather and I missed the warm, Venezuelan sun. However, I was immediately immersed in the Dutch language, and because of that, I was able to pick it up pretty well.

Looking back, I see that I've been an entrepreneur all my life and have never really worked in anyone else's company. When I arrived in the country, my man and I opened a restaurant together that served Latin American food. It was successful enough to support the opening of a second one that served Mexican food. We also owned a hotel together. We were doing well and making good money. We bought a fine home and we lived comfortably. All seemed to be going well.

Then, our daughter, Shannen, was born, which helped restore my relationship with my family. Since the country was safe to visit at that time, I returned to Venezuela two times a year. But at the same time, I was the farthest from spirituality that I've ever been in my life. I guess I just thought I didn't need it; that it didn't actually belong in my life. I've always believed in God, but don't follow an actual "religion." Instead, I believe in my relationship with God, as well as the importance to live and love myself. However, somewhere within the move to the Netherlands, I had grown not only far from my family, but far from the spirituality I knew in my childhood.

SHATTERED DREAMS

When Shannen was a baby, I decided to get an au pair to help me around the house while I was working the busy restaurant hours. I thought she was an excellent addition to my household and Shannenwas raised trilingual, speaking English, Spanish, and Dutch. After five years working in the restaurant, I wanted to spend more time at home so I decided to launch an au pair business that I could run out of the house. My business trained and placed European girls to work as live-in nannies in homes throughout the world. It was a highly successful venture and for many years I was the largest au pair service in the Netherlands.

I created an excellent training program that aspiring au pairs would fly in from around the world to attend. I served as a culture and integration coach to help the girls understand how to function in a country other than their own. The au pair world was small, so I knew people in the industry throughout the world, and I helped more than 5,500 women who came to work as au pairs from Latin American, European, African, and Asian countries.

Then the recession of 2012 hit and I saw that au pairs were one of the first line items to be slashed from so many family budgets. Little by little, I lost clients until finally, I was bankrupt.

About this time, Shannen's father, who was now doing business coaching, was overseas in China giving a workshop when he suffered two strokes. He was in a coma for two weeks and almost died. It was a trying time for us and when he came out of the stroke and returned to my Shannen and me, our relationship was never the same. I was now in serious financial difficulty, and it was then that he left us both to fend for ourselves, even though we had been together for 20 years. It wasn't long before we lost the business and the home. Shannen and I became homeless.

We were desperate. We could not travel to Venezuela, even if we could afford it, because a civil war was about to break out. Some of our friends in town told us we could stay with them, but only for two weeks. So I was very proactive and found a small, two-room flat for Shannen and I to share.

Our new home was quite a fall from the luxurious, 110 square meter home we once had. I came to face the reality that I had lost everything: my business, my home, my mate, and although I didn't realize it at the time, my hope and faith in my spirituality as well.

I fell into a deep, dark, depression that lasted eleven months. In that time, my depression led me to swallow a large amount of pills in an attempt to end my life. Luckily, I was found and saved, but I felt like a huge fraud. For days, leaving my bed was a huge undertaking. Day after day I survived this kind of life until the day I remember my best friend, and Shannen, who was 19 years old, standing in the doorway of my bedroom, crying. "This is not my mother," said Shannen. "My mother is not like this."

My daughter's words were a wakeup call. She was right. This was not me. I was lost and far from myself. I needed to come back. I realized I was not living the life I deserved. I had to do better.

Finally, I got up and took a shower. It was my first, baby step back to where I needed to be.

SPIRITUAL AGAIN

When I was in my depression, I lost the ability to connect with myself and embrace the spirituality that I had abandoned for so many years. Now I welcomed it back, and as soon as I did, my life started to change again.

It is important for us to value our spiritual self. I cannot make others happy unless I have the self-esteem to love myself.

I cannot give something to someone something that I don't give myself. You cannot love your children if you don't love yourself. You need to be a good example to them and everyone else in your life. Know that you are without limits and you can do anything. You are in charge of your mind and all you can achieve.

After experiencing tremendous spiritual growth, I decided to develop my own program for others to learn how to do the same. In my entrepreneurial ventures, I had always been a motivational trainer/coach for my au pairs and employees. I began speaking about abundance, your mind, and controlling your mindset with positivity. I pursued a coaching certification in Neurolinguistic Programming (NPL), which raises awareness of how we talk to ourselves. I also studied marketing to know how to best promote my new business, and decided to offer my counseling online, as a virtual business.

Just as my daughter gave me a wakeup call to believe in myself, now I do that for others as a business and marketing coach and mentor of women who want to transform their talent into abundance. I so enjoy helping others discover that they can achieve everything they want if they love themselves and are open to what they can co-create with the universe. To do this, you must take baby steps towards your goal. I say that nothing will come fall down to you from heaven unless you take action. It may take ten days or ten years to achieve your goal but it's all up to you.

To me, spirituality is to hear yourself, believe in yourself, and trust that you have the power to make everything that you dream of possible to achieve. It's not about what you get but what you become. So many people are disenchanted with what they do, and they feel a deep disconnection between their actions and who they are. I help them become whole again.

We live in a very negative world where we are fixed on negativity. Negativity sells. We crave the drama of the negative in the newspaper, television and internet. I believe if you see others as a victim, you take away their power to help themselves. Not to say there are not victims in the world because there are. There are poor, starving people who are not treated fairly but it's never from lack of food; it's from lack of love, fueled by our own negativity.

Love is the most happy and important energy that exists. And everything we do is done from the energy that connects us and allows us to co-create with the universe. It's easy to focus on negativity, but remember, it takes the same amount of energy to focus on good as it does to focus on the negative. So why not choose the positive? That way, you will be able to embrace the powerful spirituality within you to achieve everything you want!

REFLECTION QUESTIONS

1. How would you describe your spirituality?

2. What do you think is important for you to maintain self-love?

3. What is the next big thing you would like to co-create with the universe?

BIOGRAPHY

Marielys Ávila is a business and marketing-spiritual coach and mentor of women who want to transform their talent into abundance and achieve the thriving business of their dreams. In 2012, she was bankrupt and didn't have enough money for groceries. She went on to build a multiple, six-figure company that helps women become clear about their goals, define a marketing strategy to follow, and develop a winning mentality.

Marielys is a lifelong entrepreneur who relocated to Caracas, Venezuela to Holland to start life in a new country. There, she launched an au pair agency that helped thousands of women around the world, in 44 different countries with 58 nationalities.

Today, she offers her coaching to help her clients increase their ability to get the results they want through the spirituality and marketing, eliminate economic ups and downs of your life, and end their professional dissatisfaction. Through her virtual business, marielysavila. com, she offers ebooks, courses, and individual coaching sessions to clients. She still resides in Holland.

Marielys Ávila
team@marielysavila.nl
Instagram: @marielyscoach

Rubmary Díaz Marcano

"We must have important things on the horizon and visualize them every day."

Storytelling is not my forte. But here is my story; the story of a Latina in Dutch lands.

I am Rubmary Díaz Marcano. They call me Rub, for short. The nickname comes from the first three letters of my father's name, Rubén Emiliano Díaz. Now you will probably read it correctly: Rub.

Being part of this first edition of *Today's Inspired Latina* in Europe is a true honor that carries a huge responsibility. Inspiring someone is easy, but is it possible? According to Google, "to inspire" means to wake up or cause a feeling, or an impression in a mood. I'm hoping to inspire you to take that leap to launch your projects, your dreams, your goals, step by step, and with an objective to grow both personally and professionally.

BEYOND BORDERS

I'm the mother of a boy named Leonardo Rubén, born in Spain and the wife of a wonderful and hardworking man named Carlos. I have been away from my home country for several years. We have lived in three different countries, with three different cultures, and three different languages, and the only thing that remained unchanged in my life was me. I always was, am, and will be that Rub: fighter, warrior, and imperfect person, because perfection doesn't exist, and (as people say) it's better done than perfect.

We lived in three countries: Spain, the United Kingdom, and Holland. All three are wonderful, with their own pros and cons, and there are things I miss about each one.

For example, from Spain, I miss the weather, my father's visits, working in a law firm, going out with the Latino community, and speaking my language. From the United Kingdom, specifically Wales, I miss seeing the sheep behind the house, breathing fresh air, sharing with friends who are now like family, the green, and the tranquility. As for Holland, I am still gradually discovering it since I currently live there, at least until I move again!

Reading online, I found this phrase: "You don't miss the things, you miss the moments you lived in that specific place, whether with friends, family, or by yourself." That is true for me.

Now, as I'm a digitally savvy woman, I searched the internet again to see what Google tell us about resilience and I found, "Resilience is the ability of a person or group to recover from adversity to continue projecting the future. Sometimes, under difficult circumstances or traumas, it allows the development of resources that were latent, and that the individual(s) didn't know existed until now." This definition helps illustrate my story.

If you are reading this story and are a Latina outside your

borders, you will know how hard it is to be away from the family. I think that for me, it has been the most difficult thing, especially being away from my father, who visited me a few times in Spain. Honestly, he didn't visit enough, but I was always grateful for his presence.

A FATHER'S LEGACY

Unfortunately, my father passed away recently and it has been hard for me, being thousands of kilometers away. The situation in Venezuela is not new, and conditions there aggravated my father's health. He was a man of principle, a man full of knowledge without having gone through college. For this reason, I want to honor him in this book.

His influence over me is ever-present. He was the most important person in my life and helped me pay for my law degree. As a good father, he supported me in all my activities. Many memories come to mind, like my father bringing food to my catechism workshop, how he never liked taking pictures and covered himself with his hands, how he usually slept in a hammock and maybe in a bed only a few times when he visited me, and so many more memories I will cherish in mind and heart until we meet again.

My father would tell me to read, study, and learn, and for this reason, I do it whenever I can because I also have several roles as a mother, woman, and entrepreneur. The pressure of wanting to do everything is counterproductive, and I have felt it in my flesh. It's important to have a space of self-care where you do activities that include relaxation and little things in life that enhance the being.

Our communication via telephone was constant, fluid, and now I need to hear his voice, understand him, learn from him. I sometimes feel that I didn't learn enough, but am happy to have been his daughter and to have given him the best I could.

No one learns from the experiences of others, but they help motivate and inspire us, as I told you earlier in this story. If your father is alive, call him every day. Spend quality time with him, surprise him, and make him happy, because it's the most important thing we can do: BE HAPPY.

Overcoming my father's loss is difficult for me, but I don't feel that he is gone. He is still there, when I lie down, when I get up, when I walk, when I eat. I've always followed my father and will continue to do so because he left his legacy.

When I heard about his passing, my mother was visiting in Holland. She was very supportive, and I will always be grateful for how things happened. They say things always turn out for the best. It is no less true that my mother also supported me, as well as my stepfather. I'll always be grateful to them. Thank the supreme being you believe in, be it God, be it energy, or anything else.

My dad was a humanitarian. He never rested from helping those in need and he read books daily and seemed to know everything. That was something he tried to instill in me. He told me that a good lawyer has to read a lot. It's never too late to acquire reading habits. I will honor him by reading this first edition of *Today's Inspired Latina* in Europe, with the stories of all the other women who are included. May my *viejito* (old man) rest in eternity at 82, Rubén Emiliano Díaz Moreno, who was a politician, trade unionist, advocate of the working class, agrarian, and promoter of the Trade Union Movement.

The legacy of my father was both materialistic and non-materialistic, and I want to share the best of what he taught me:

- Be a woman with resilience.
- Be a woman with values.
- Be a woman with principles.
- Be a woman who knows how to forgive.
- Be a woman who asks for forgiveness.
- Be a woman who prays.
- Be a woman who inspires.
- Be a good person, mother, and wife.

A LATINA LEGACY

Together, my father and I created a motto, "Success is achieved with work and faith," for my speech at the 1st Face-to-Face Emigrate and Undertake event in Spain. I want to reflect on this phrase. Honest work dignifies us as a people and as human beings, always helping each other and creating connections that contribute to humanity.

We must work with passion, but also attached to reality, aligned in mind, body, and spirit to make it easier. Remember that it's you who can decide to do it or not, in order to influence others. It's time to work and intertwine the concept with faith, as my father said. Pure magic will happen, since faith moves mountains. To believe in God is to believe in yourself and your project.

Often people tell me, "Rub you inspire and motivate me." I answer, "Thank you, so now it's time to build strength and start reaching your short and long-term goals. Work for your dreams and you will inspire many as well."

Every time I receive these messages and beautiful words from people at a higher level, I feel that I'm on the right track. My work gives me a clear roadmap to follow, so I can continue working and helping others.

To succeed, you have to work and do what you like. Many times we work on what we don't like, but in order to change that environment, we must gain self-knowledge and see what we can do to change that reality.

Dream.

Create your reality.

Do it.

Latinas in the world are leaving a legacy. Try to let people remember you for what you made them feel, not for what you won or lost. It's pleasing to make people feel. Emotions are conjugated, like joy, sadness, and anger. It's normal to feel, but NEVER allow emotions to dominate you. And above all, say NO, when you don't want to do something with someone.

The best thing that is happening now is that you are reading my story! I hope it will inspire you to live abroad, perform fully as a person and a professional, and not die trying. We are inspiring

Latinas with perseverance, dedication, and respect for each other. All our stories are important, so tell yours to the world. Resonate with it. Behind every story, there may be sacrifices and endless other events which can strengthen and move us all.

This is how we must continue along the road outside our borders. We must have important things on the horizon and visualize them every day. Imagine them, including the details, and create true and valuable connections where you can feel free and be yourself. These relationships will be your greatest treasure.

Abroad, find support and be part of a tribe where you feel included. Everything won't be perfect. There will be friction and you may not agree with everyone, but you will be able to learn from each life lesson.

Life is short. Live it, feel it, fall, and get up, without caring what people will say. I think that is the key. Life is a gift.

The challenges of living far away and using another language, like I do, gets difficult. I have struggled but I have created digital businesses and I've helped others do the same. I want to continue creating unique spaces to leave a legacy.

But there is also something I want to emphasize. Entrepreneur mothers have a hard job, and let's not forget single mothers. When we are mothers, we not only take care of the children and look after the business, we also have to build value, create effective plans and manage the resources we have in the best possible way in order to obtain results. If we don't get the expected results, we need to measure, analyze, and move forward. Never backwards, not even to gain momentum, say my dear Venezuelans.

On a professional level, I want to thank my mentor Verónica Sosa, from whom I have learned much. We must lead from the heart. It's not only what we can do, but what we are doing. The purpose of the S.H.E. Hispanic Entrepreneurs manifesto, which I am honored to promote as an ambassador in Holland, tells us to be yourself, know yourself, and be authentic. Be generous, work with purpose, be "coachable" and let yourself be guided.

Our business plans flow through our ideas, so we must be integral in mind, body, and spirit. We must share to have. We must think that together, we can grow more. Keep your balance and leave a legacy, a business with a purpose.

When branding, know your business. In marketing, publicize your business. Make smart associations by partnering with people who add something to your business. Cooperate; it will always be more effective to complement each other than to compete with each other.

I also want to thank Jacqueline Camacho Ruiz, a visionary, entrepreneurial woman, full of energy, for allowing me to tell my story to the world and open doors for me.

May the entrepreneurs live, may empowering Latinas live. Let's keep leaving legacies, walking with strength so nobody stops us. May the magic never end.

powerful woman.

REFLECTION QUESTIONS

1. Do you believe you would learn more from living abroad?

2. How do you value things with more intensity?

3. Are you prepared to recover easily from adversity?

BIOGRAPHY

Rubmary Díaz Marcano is a Venezuelan, visionary, adventurous entrepreneur, and social network lover. She lives in the Netherlands but has previously lived in Great Britain and Spain.

Rub has a proven, three-year, international track record for event management, leading and coordinating events, workshops, seminars, and congresses. She is a strong networker, and is social media-driven with a passionate, action-oriented personality.

She develops digital projects for herself and women who want to start their own adventures. She founded "Extranjería 2.0", an immigration consultancy service with specialized lawyers, "Emigrar y Emprender," a periodic entrepreneurial event, and "To Be Emprendedor," a service aimed at helping entrepreneurs boost their brands. Also, with Yamily Figueroa, she co-organized "Reinvéntate en el Extranjero," an online community helping professionals start their careers in foreign countries.

Rub is a Netherlands ambassador for "Seminario para Hispanas Emprendedoras," an event for Spanish-speaking, entrepreneurial women, based in Central Europe and founded by her mentor, Verónica Sosa. She holds a Bachelor of Law degree from the Santa María University, Venezuela, recognized by the University of Alcalá, Spain, a master's degree in procedural law from the National University of Rosario, Argentina, and a master's degree in sustainable human development from the University of Girona, Spain.

Rubmary Díaz Marcano
hello@rubdiaz.com
Social Media: @rubdiazm

Virginia Callizaya Terceros

"If you wish hard enough, dreams do come true,
because to dream is free."

When I was growing up in Bolivia, people always asked me the typical childhood question, "What will you be when you grow up?" I used to answer, "I will marry a foreigner and go to Venice on our honeymoon," although I had no idea where in the world Venice was. I just knew that Venice was called the city of love. I also answered that I would become a businesswoman because as my aunties used to say, "If you wish hard enough, dreams do come true, because to dream is free."

I grew up in a beautiful family. I was the coddled one. I had two soccer-player brothers and one younger, quiet, and relaxed sister. My mother ruled at home, while my father laid the foundations of our future. My parents instilled values and principles in us, and we were given plenty of love. My father was methodical and disciplined, and so we learned to play chess before we could read or write. We spent long evenings involved in family competitions until we would literally fall asleep over the chessboard.

The prize or punishment to whims, messes, and mischief

as a kid was, depending on the situation, to play chess with my brother Andrés, who had already won the children's national chess championship at a very early age. I feel nostalgic when I recall those games with my dad when he would say "think and use the strategies we've studied." When he was angry, every once in a blue moon, he used to tell us, "This science-game and its logic will help you throughout your life, you'll see." Sometimes I felt so powerless, I could cry. Later, I understood why.

Mamma was a tireless fighter, always advocating for people in need. She taught us to share the very little we had. Usually, I got upset when I came home and found a stranger. She told us those people did not have a place to spend the night in the city and so she would invite them to stay with us. My mother gave everything she could to the needy with love and respect.

I learned from my parents to be kind, to help others and, above all, to "not let your left hand know what your right hand is doing." They have always been my inspiration and support and their discipline helped me a lot with my studies and work, although I had no time to do the things my peers were doing.

My dad retired the same year I graduated from school. I completed a secretarial course so I could quickly find a job and help my parents afford my university tuition.

LIFE CHECKMATE

I started working as a secretary for a privately-owned company located in the city of La Paz. Simultaneously, I was studying at the public university to become an auditor. After three months at the company, and being a naïve college junior, I discovered a significant case of embezzlement by a high-grade employee at the company. I was also able to prove it. This, added to my enthusiasm for the job, led me to receive a memorandum on the same day notifying me I was assigned to the position of Company Administrator. By that time, I was two months away from being 18 years old—barely of age to be performing the responsibilities of that role.

Every step I took, I remembered the wise words of my father and the useful strategies learned on those long evenings in front of the chessboard, looking for a checkmate.

After a while, and given my consistency at work, I was promoted to the position of General Manager. My determination and devotion yielded results. I accomplished every goal with the help of my university teachers, who indirectly became company consultants without knowing it. Eventually, our company managed to capture an advantageous position in a competitive, industry market.

I was now in a position of tremendous responsibility, which was not easy within the context of a macho culture. I was directing and giving orders to men on a daily basis.

With my acquired expertise and lots of hard work, I opened my own importing company, motivated by, and at the same time grateful towards, the owners of the company I had helped save from bankruptcy. It was not easy. However, I truly believe there is an inner force—and I have experienced it--that becomes stronger when you work on something you created from scratch.

It makes you feel totally empowered. It was difficult to pave the way to success and build a reputation as a serious competitor in the marketplace, but there was no alternative and no way back; I had to pay the bank.

Launching the business brought me satisfaction but also physical problems, such as ulcers developed by stress. At 22 years old, my search for perfectionism landed me in the hospital emergency room. The problem could be traced to my work and studies, and it was a sign I needed to stop to redirect and reorganize my life.

EVERYTHING FOR LOVE

Between all my comings and goings, I met a handsome Belgium guy and fell in love. I decided to get married and leave everything I had achieved behind, despite the strong opposition of my family. My dream as a child came true; everything happened as I had envisioned.

We decided to live in Belgium, a totally different culture for me. At the beginning, I was scared, as any Latin girl coming to live in Europe might be.

I had left all my entrepreneurship behind for love. At that time, my career, and even my driver's license, were not valid in Belgium. I didn't know the language, which I had to learn from zero. It was very difficult for me since I'd gone from being a totally independent woman to becoming fully dependent on my husband. Only the profound love I felt for him made things a little bit easier.

Our marriage was blessed with two sons—Antoon and Mateo—who have always been good reasons to remain in the country. My husband and I started running a geriatric care facility called Rustoord Vlaspand. It was a brand new business for me.

Thus, years went by while preparing baby bottles, changing diapers, studying the language, and trying with difficulty to assimilate. Although I already spoke French, Dutch was the prevailing language in Antwerp, where I lived. This would prompt bursts of nostalgia and a strong desire to someday return to my country and to my family, who I missed so much.

FACING ADVERSITY

Some years ago, I got a call that pierced my heart. It was bad news from my home country. My dear mother was sick and in the hospital. All my brothers, my sister, and me, along with my dad, were there with her to say goodbye. We lost her due to medical negligence, a typical mistake in our underdeveloped country.

My mom, an entrepreneur herself, had managed to fund a soccer school for kids in need for which she received an award from government authorities. Her death was a pain I could not overcome. I was heartbroken. I cannot explain what it was like to see so many kids crying for her.

I came back to Belgium feeling miserable and angry with Bolivia. And to make matters worse, after two months, and without warning, my husband somehow also decided to leave me, the kids, and the company project.

I could not believe what was happening to me. Sometimes

everything looks perfect and you see people in similar or worse situations, and you think that could never happen to you. Yet in less than three months, I had lost my mother and my husband. I could not help but ask, what will I do? I was alone with the kids, at a complicated age, with a house to maintain and a geriatric care facility to run that was about to go bankrupt, which was something I did not even know about.

Divorce was the word that my daddy once told me was not in his dictionary. At first, I was ashamed, but I shouldn't have been! I had devoted 15 years to my marriage, and I was proud of that.

In that harsh moment, I had two possibilities: I could sit and cry until I was mired in depression, or I would be brave and take the bull by the horns, which was easier said than done. I did both. I cried a lot, though at night when no one could see me. In front of people and the whole world, I would be as strong as ever. We were very well known where we lived, and I had no private life. My life was public domain, which made everything even more painful.

My friends who were lawyers and finance professionals suggested that I file for bankruptcy or sell the company with all the debts at a low price. I had many offers from important businessmen for the geriatric care facility business. Some of them even dared say a foreign woman could not be in charge and control of a company all alone. They only wanted to scare me so that I would sell the company I had worked so hard to build. I had devoted myself to the business and it had taught me many skills that I would not have discovered anywhere else. Instead of making me feel bad, all the intimidation encouraged me to continue, with the wisdom of my brother, who had recently received his PhD. He employed his emotional skills to underpin my entrepreneurial, brave, fighting spirit.

"Pursue your ideals as you have always done," he told me on the other end of the telephone line. And this message went straight to my brain and renewed my energy.

Daddy told me not to be afraid because Mom was taking care of me from heaven. After all, I was not alone. I had two kids, many older people to take care of and many co-workers that would be unemployed if I gave up. So I followed my instinct and fought for what I really wanted.

I worked around the clock. I did the work of four people to save on wages. It was a constant daily struggle. Virginia, the entrepreneur, was back in business and she would not quit.

I refreshed myself by completing a postgraduate course for geriatric care facility directors. The course was very difficult. The laws governing the activity are very strict and complex, and training is essential because of the high standards of quality that are required. But I have a prevailing advantage that has to do with the loving and gentle manners we Latinas have. I defended my thesis before the panel on the same day of the election of the first Belgium Prime Minister of Italian origin—Elio Di Rupo—who spoke Dutch even worse than me. So I started with a joke by saying "I also dream I can become Prime Minister one day." We laughed a lot (Latin charm) and I passed the examination. How wonderful!

Since then, I work every day to give my elderly residents a decent life with plenty of love, something very needed in this cold country. My work is my passion. Every day I wake up and look to the sky and pray, "Please, help me to help."

Currently, I have a top-notch professional team. WZC Vlaspand has become one of the best senior living communities in Flanders, thanks to the help of my older son, Antoon, who is currently my right-hand man and successor.

I dream of funding a similar geriatric care facility in Bolivia. Unfortunately, elderly people in my home country have few resources. I would like to offer them the best quality of life for the rest of their life. At present, to make the dream come true, I only have a piece of land and lots of hopes.

In the meanwhile, I will go on dreaming. Because to dream is free and everything is possible if you truly desire it.

REFLECTION QUESTIONS

1. Are you doing what you really want to do or what others want you to do?

2. If you could choose anywhere to live, where would it be?

3. What past choices would you change now?

BIOGRAPHY

Virginia Callizaya Terceros is a visionary entrepreneur who likes to help others and speaks five different languages. Virginia has a degree in financial audit from Mayor de San Andrés de La Paz University.

She started her career as an administrator at American Tools Bolivia. Later, she founded her own company called Falcon Trading SRL and also got the inspiration to start her second company, a wooden toy factory. Virginia is also currently the General Director of WZC VLASPAND SERVICE FLATS, located in Westerlo province Antwerp, Belgium.

Virginia was born in La Paz, Bolivia. She is divorced from her ex-husband, Antoon Huylebroeck, but they remain friends and take trips together with their two children, Antoon Andres and Mateo. In her free time, she gives Spanish lessons, enjoys traveling, reading, and playing chess.

Virginia Callizaya Terceros
virginia3ros@yahoo.es
0032 478 256 805

Silvia Tapia

"Life remains a privilege, even when there are moments of darkness."

If you've ever been told that you're a miracle, let me reaffirm it: yes, you are. If you have ever been told that you're something other than love, believe me that's a lie; you're real, and only love is real.

It's amazing how the universe conspires to let miracles manifest, no matter how adverse the circumstances are. I was born two months early, in the middle of the mountains, where there were no doctors, no hospitals, and no incubators. My parents kept me warm with hot water bottles. My father says that I was so small I could fit in the palm of his hand, yet that tiny girl survived.

Years later, I was a happy child, the daughter of peasants. I climbed trees, rode horses, took care of sheep, and learned to cultivate the land, all while questioning myself: what's behind the clouds? What's beyond the horizon? And why do two people who fight so much live together?

Years later, when I was a teenager, I set some goals. These goals were accompanied by illusion, but also insecurity; aspiration, but also the vulnerability suffered by those who don't know who they are. No matter how much you know or how much knowledge you accumulate, if you don't know who you are, it won't help you much. You can learn a lot about land, but a breeding ground for you is you.

IN LOVE, FOR LOVE

I was 23 years old, but my thoughts were still those of an adolescent. I embarked on a beautiful love story full of illusion, with life goals that originally were not mine; my dream was my husband's proposal. I agreed to join him in his dream.

The first four months were fabulous, and I was very much in love. It was never my plan to fall in love; I didn't believe in it. I knew what it felt like to have a boyfriend, but my dating relationships did not last. I just dated casually; I wasn't looking for anything serious. So when things got serious, or someone proposed to me, I cut off the relationship and fled. Marriage didn't fit into my projected life plan. There was only room for one adopted child, a good job, a beautiful house, and that was it.

But when my husband came into my life, I said goodbye to my personal plan. Now we both embarked on his plan, and his dreams were my dreams. I no longer wanted to adopt a child; I adopted a life plan in which I was given a daughter and two sons, who were not adopted, but were born from my womb, from our love. Everything seemed to flow, but after a while it seemed like he was no longer enjoying having me along with him, and suddenly, I realized that my life was not pink, but gray.

After a fabulous start, my life lost its charm. It increasingly bothered me until I found myself in deep despair. I felt that there was no way to redeem my life, so I opted for the easy exit: a suicide attempt. I tried not just once, but twice, but those attempts failed, and here I am. Afterwards, my life was still gray and my frustration grew, filling me with resentment, bitterness, jealousy, and helplessness, until one day, I was diagnosed with cervical cancer.

My life is a constant transformation along a path of transcendence. Thank God, I transcended. As I always say, "God healed me through alternative means and four disciplines" that led me to personal transformation, which continues today. Through discipline in my life, my cancer transcended and my consciousness began to awaken.

FINDING THE MISSION

I felt that I had a mission because I assumed that God wouldn't be rescuing me from so many circumstances without a reason. Surely my life had a purpose, but what was it? I didn't know yet! So, I decided to prepare professionally to be ready to carry out a mission.

At that point, I only had a high school education and a career as a shorthand clerk. So I resumed my professional training while raising my three children, ages 8, 10 and 13. I was aware of my responsibility to them and my home, but by then, my marriage was deteriorating. On one occasion my husband told me, "Don't be crazy! If you didn't study when you were growing up, forget about it now." I didn't count on his support and decided to move forward in my purpose and transcend any barrier put in my path.

Fortunately, through my work, God supported and always provided for me. I managed to pay not only for my education but for childcare, since my husband would contribute for food, but would not support my absence from the children by paying for a babysitter. By mid-career, I had established a financial business. By the end of my career, I had earned the respect and recognition not only of my children, but of my husband, as well.

By then, I felt I no longer needed support, because in some way, I had already shown myself how much I could accomplish on my own. My husband started picking me up from school along with our children, and being attentive to me, which had not happened in a long time. Isn't that interesting? By then, I was no longer interested in fighting. My education in neurolinguistic programming and other disciplines had helped me a lot and I also didn't have time to fight.

Later, my mother also developed cancer and I had the privilege of accompanying her through the process, supporting her until she transcended it. I told her the same thing that I tell every woman in the world who deals with that blessed disease: "Cancer is not synonymous with death; it's an area of opportunity, and when you transcend cancer, nothing and nobody will stop you."

I want to clarify that I don't believe that it's necessary to generate a cancer to transcend and then realize that we have a mission in life. I think that once our consciousness awakens, it speaks to us, and even if it speaks softly, we can hear it. That way, we can discern our mission in life, which is our "what," and "what are we here for?"

So how do you wake up without having to endure the extremes that I did? Well, for me it was not the cancer itself, but rather the discipline of transformation, which as I said, was four points of discipline. I changed...

1. My way of thinking
2. My way of eating
3. My way of life, and;
4. My way of looking at life

How could this have had such an impact on my life and my health? Thoughts cannot always be easily changed because it requires us to care for our nutrition, which is not just our physical nourishment. I first learned and understood this while dealing with cancer. I also learned about the synergies of plants and that we are spirit, soul, and body. As I postulated in my book, *The Privilege of Living*, we have to take care of nourishing ourselves in these three areas of our integral person and remember that nutrition enters through our five senses. So being aware of what we eat is taking care of what we taste, what we see, what we hear, what we smell, what we touch, and who we interact with since the vibration of the environment has a high impact on our lives.

My thoughts are generated based on what enters my brain, and what enters my brain will depend on my belief system. Therefore, everything that I'm exposed to and communicating with are the beliefs that I harbor and at that moment, they will motivate my point of view that in turn will impact my information processing and generate a type of thought. With those thoughts, I will develop other actions, and continue this way to generate a lifestyle.

AWAKENING

So how do we awaken? In summary, the answer is in love and with love, because before getting cancer, I didn't love or think about myself. I think that my plan of having a good job, getting a nice house, and adopting a child was a scheme that looked good to the world, but hadn't developed from love or for love. It had developed from ego and fear.

Before embarking on the journey called family with my husband, I thought I could avoid dealing with men because my parent's relationship was violent and a poor example of marriage. I didn't want to repeat the pattern. On the other hand, my husband wanted to have children made from the love he said he felt for me, but I had never thought about getting pregnant or having children. My mother had 14 pregnancies and since I was the third one, I had already dealt with many babies; I didn't need more. I appreciated them, but unlike my parents, I knew that they required a lot of attention. So my fear of repeating patterns, my fear of marriage, and many other fears accompanied me on this adventure. Cancer was no accident.

Now, when evaluating my life path, I observe that my fears and beliefs acquired in my family environment led me to think in certain ways, in certain circumstances, and to make certain decisions. However, what I did for love, not out of fear, endures and gives me satisfaction despite the dark moments that my fears can generate. Everything I did and decided in love has led me to growth and stimulated my inner resolve to reach the next level, or the next goal.

Of course, my husband also had fears that certainly influenced some of his decisions, but that's another story. I will only tell you that today it is very rewarding when he says, "Thanks to you, I'm a better person," while I answer, "And thanks to you, I am too."

In spite of the very difficult moments that we have gone through in our relationship, my bout with cancer and his with diabetes, we have both grown a lot and feel blessed in our relationship. This leads me to believe that it was worth leaving my personal plan to embark on a collective plan, where the community is my husband, me, and now my children. However, this story is not over yet. I know that even if on the way we decide to separate, today we have the maturity to do it with love, respecting and blessing ourselves, and knowing that if such a decision is made, it's because it will bless our lives even more. That is why I dare to say that anything that blesses the couple will bless the children, because the tree cannot be robust and full of wisdom without its branches enjoying that prosperity.

Today, I live in the here and now. I have used many life tools and developed and taught many more. Even with all this, sometimes situations take me by surprise and circumstances shake me, but like James Allen says, "Circumstances don't make me, they only manifest me." As soon as I become consciously aware, I become my observer and the situation ends up being a blessing for my life, because I can create chaos, or transcendence and balance. Life remains a privilege, even when there are moments of darkness. Thus, from my perspective, everything is summed up to that Law of Love, which is not merely human, but a spiritual law, from which all universal laws and more descend.

Today, the vast majority know that we don't come to suffer, but to live in fullness. The problem is that we don't believe it and knowing is not enough to manifest it; you need to believe we are in connection with the source. We are prosperity.

REFLECTION QUESTIONS

1. What fears do you have in life that you need to transcend?

2. How do you nourish yourself in Spirit, Soul, and Body?

3. Which of the four disciplines in life would most greatly affect your happiness?

BIOGRAPHY

Silvia Garcia Tapia is a life coach, financial advisor, and business consultant. She was born on June 20, 1972 in the town of Las Minas in the Mexican state of Veracruz. She is licensed in business administration and human development.

Silvia has spoken internationally on various topics and is the author of the book, *The Privilege of Living*.

Silvia Tapia
elprivilegiodevivir@hotmail.com
+52 1 228 160 8997

Estefania Roa

"Don't allow your past to destroy you; allow it to transform you and make you stronger."

Even since I was inside my mother's womb, I have felt lonely. Perhaps many readers will find that sentence ironic, but what I mean is that there was a time in my life that I thought my mom must have suffered a lot when she was carrying me in her womb. I imagined that she felt vulnerable, sad, and lonely. It made me think about how hard it is to bring someone into this world when society is against you, and when the person who was part of that procreation also leaves you. My dad evidently wanted nothing to do with me.

My mom, being a single, young mother without financial stability, decided to leave me with my grandparents so that she could seek a better life for our family. She decided to pursue the American Dream.

FOR WANT OF FAMILY

I was not a child who wanted toys and I didn't have many of them. All I really wanted, with all my heart, was to have a family. I wanted to have someone who would tell me I was important, I was loved, and to have that mother who would walk into my school events feeling proud of me. I wished I was able to understand why I was left behind, why they (my parents) didn't want to be part of my life. For many years, I felt guilty about their absence.

At the age of five, I remember asking my grandma to make desserts and Jell-O for me to sell on the street. I would go door to door selling tamales and delivering dinner plates to the neighbors, and I had a part-time job after school working for a man who sold chickens on the street. I spent hours listening to his bible stories, and he taught me how to assist customers in the kindest way. Even at a very young age, I would do anything that was within my reach to earn some extra cash.

For many years, I carried a secret with me--a secret of being a victim of sexual abuse. I was only six years old and didn't say anything until I was 11; I was scared to death and felt ashamed of my body and person. I thought that I would be judged and that my family would not believe me. However, once I spoke out, I felt liberated and free. But I still felt I had a brick of pain in my tower of sorrow.

Eventually, I reunited with my mother. I could hardly remember how she looked, and again, I had created a wonderful expectation of how our life would be now that we were back together. When traveling on that plane to America, I thought my life would finally be normal. I'd have a mom, a dad - her husband-- and siblings to take care of and play with me. It sounds like I finally had a happy story. Except that I didn't. My mother and her husband battled alcoholism, and so began a difficult episode in my life. Neither my siblings nor I were important, and our achievements and dreams didn't matter. I hung out with the wrong crowd, and no one even knew. Sadly, their alcoholism tore us apart, leaving a horrible scar in my heart, unable to build any happy stories or memories.

LIFE AND DECISIONS

Life is all about decisions... what we decide to be, who we decide to be with, and who we decide to forgive.

Around the time I was 12 years old, I decided to find my biological father. It was not a hard task. I found him and wrote a beautiful letter for him, pouring my heart out. I repeated in my head over and over again what I would say when I saw him, how I would smile, and how I would use the manners my grandparents had taught me. And so, I went to meet him. I wore the best outfit I could find and did my hair as if I was going to a very important event. I thought he would smile at me, hug me, and ask me for forgiveness, and of course I would forgive him. I cherished the thought of him being a part of my life.

But it wasn't like that. He didn't smile; he sarcastically laughed at my presence and told me that my mother and I were liars. He said no one should ever find out about my existence and that he was sorry, but he didn't want anything to do with me. That was just another brick to add to my tower of pain and sorrow.

When I was 12, I met a boy who was 17, and I seriously thought I was in love, despite my entire family disapproving of our relationship. Nonetheless, I figured out a way to see him and be with him, and at the age of 14, I was pregnant.

My family thought my life was over. People felt sorry for me which was starting to seem like a normal thing. My friends stopped being my friends, and some of their parents thought I was a bad influence on them. When people referred to me, they would describe me as a failure.

At the age of 15, I gave birth to a little boy. I cried for many nights, completely shattered and afraid, feeling responsible for that little life. I had no clue what to do with him. He was real. He cried and didn't sleep. He was hungry every two hours and I was in much physical and emotional pain.

At the age of 16, I went to live with my son's father. I was working full time and wasn't going to school anymore. I cannot blame my son's father for everything that went wrong between us; we were both so young. He made mistakes, I made mistakes, and it just didn't work out.

What I do know is that no matter what, I would never abandon my child. I looked that little boy in the eyes and decided to start building a castle for him. Enough with the tower of sorrow and pain. I took all my bricks of pain and utilized them to form a strong foundation, giving myself and my child another chance in life, a hope for a better life.

For many years, I was lost with no guidance, no mentorship, and just wondering what I could do to survive. I had abandoned my education to provide for my son. One thing I knew is that I was never, ever going to give up, and after several attempts to finish high school, I completed my GED. No one knew, and no one cheered for me. It was my own responsibility to become the best version of myself I could be. I accepted the idea that I didn't need anyone to feel proud of me.

I went through several jobs with only with one purpose- to learn more. I cleaned houses, I sold anything and everything door to door, business to business, at one point carrying luggage cases full of merchandise in one hand and a car seat in the other. I was at many multi-level companies, worked at a gas station, sold insurance, and became licensed. I did everything I could to provide for my child.

RELEASING THE PAST

I was determined to learn everything I could about financial services, including tax preparation and banking, and so I did. I realized that in life we have to knock on many doors, and eventually one will open.

I prayed for a sign. I knew God would provide for us and that his timing would be perfect.

I have gone through many stages in my life and the most important one to me has been the stage of forgiveness. Learning to accept and embrace my past and reality is what changed me the most. I forgave everyone who had caused me pain. I forgave myself for making bad decisions and for allowing myself to get hurt.

Slowly, things started to improve for me. I believed in myself, and I knew my life was meant for something greater. I built a relationship with a loving man and decided to make him part of our lives. I fought for our love and we made a family together. That picture from my childhood finally started to look real. We even got a dog.

For the first time in my life, I started to feel grateful. I found people that inspired me, people who told me I was smart and capable, and for once, I started to believe that maybe I was smart, capable, and able to do great things. I spent my time reading, researching, calming my soul, working on my inner peace, and creating ideas to have a better future. It's when we get to the root of why it's so hard to release and forgive that we can finally begin to release the power that unforgiveness holds over us.

Six years ago, I was content working where I was employed. However, I felt there was more for me to do. I kept thinking, I will not settle, *I will learn more, I will do more*. One day my step-dad, someone who I didn't have much of a relationship with back then, asked me to leave my job, to invest all our life savings and to join him in a business venture on a project that held an uncertain future.

The business was bankrupt, had three employees, and was completely in debt. It was a business idea that only someone with a big vision and heart would be able to comprehend. I decided to take the risk because sometimes, the things that seem the most difficult, end up being the most rewarding and transforming if you only give them a chance. I find it important to hold on to my dreams and to never stop believing in myself, even if the entire world doesn't.

Sometimes you can build relationships that become amazing

and can transform you, like the one I now have with my step-dad and my beautiful mom. I prayed that one day they would cure themselves and today, they are going strong and have been alcohol-free for three years.

For me, it took holding onto all my past experiences to become a better person, to fight every day to figure out a way to make that company succeed and to recreate something from the ashes. I was able to rescue my hopes and dreams, be a good example for my children, and to scream out loud to the world that I once had the option to be a victim, but I decided to be an entrepreneur. In other words, don't allow your past to define you, destroy you, or defeat you; only allow it the power to transform you and make you stronger."

Today, after six years of that decision, we are a proud, minority-owned business. My family and I have transformed the company's values, following a better path. We are creating a mission within our community to fireproof our buildings and we're going strong providing employment for more than 18 families and 25 employees. Our vision is to take our company to the highest standards of quality, inspire those who surround us, and create a better life for many people.

I now have a new story to write and it looks nothing like my past. I will not settle; this is only the beginning of an interesting chapter.

Nice to meet you, I am Estefania Roa.

REFLECTION QUESTIONS

1. How much more forgiveness, compassion, kindness and love would you give if you knew that it could multiply within you?

2. How can you let your difficult past experiences transform you into a better version of yourself?

3. Have you ever experienced a "Metanoia?" (a transformative change of heart or spiritual conversion?)

BIOGRAPHY

Estefania Roa is a life and business coach. Her mission is to help people see a vision of their lives and then create the happiness and wealth they desire by taking charge of their thoughts.

Estefania is the founder of HOLA HAPPY foundation, a nonprofit organization that works with individuals to make a difference in the quality of life of people who are often forgotten. She is also the chief executive officer at L.B. Hall Enterprises, Inc. an established and accepted spray applied fireproofing and insulation contractor and minority-owned business in Elk Grove Village.

Estefania Roa
847-708-4554
eroa@lbhall.com

Marita Valdizan

"We need to see the light in every storm."

As I write this, a simple crochet hook and wire are at my side. It makes me unique, like all of us are. We are all unique and gorgeous, and all of us deserve to be happy. In the past, I have felt like an outsider, like I didn't fit in anywhere. Now that I'm 44 years old, I am knitting dreams for everyone who needs them. I am a simple mother and woman, with a crazy and creative mind. I love to share my work with others and my life's passion is to always have the ability to create art wherever I may be. I believe in God, so I believe he created me as an artist so I could create magic for others with my hands. My tools to do this include a simple mixed media technique and a crochet hook and a wire. I encourage you to find your own tools to create magic!

THE BUDDING ARTIST

Growing up in Peru, my parents and my grandfather had the biggest influence on me because without them, I wouldn't be the person I am today. They raised me to have values, be proud of my country, and love my roots.

Both my grandfather and my father were physicians who

loved to serve others. I remember when my father told me how much my grandfather loved providing psychiatric services to patients and going above and beyond for them for free. He cared for his patients as he would for his family, even taking them to his home for lunch or dinner. My family influenced me to always share my time and passion with others, regardless of my chosen profession.

In school, I never felt like I really fit in and I had low self-esteem. I overcame constant bullying throughout my school years, which ultimately helped me when I became a mother. I was able to teach my children to never give up on their dreams and to not allow their life experience to define who they are. I believe God allowed me to experience every moment in order to be able to love and show other women that everyone is powerful and deserves love. My art is unique and is made with love and passion, created for them alone. As new obstacles arise, my art becomes my therapy.

As a child, I gave my small creations as gifts to my family. As young as nine years old, I took classes for different art techniques. I started teaching ceramic classes at the age of 12. My income helped my parents, and I continued studying art after high school in order to support myself.

After a few years of studying art, I also took a job as an office receptionist at the Supreme Court of Justice in Peru. I worked there for more than three years. Every day, I heard people's stories about wanting social justice and it certainly impacted my focus on my art, my paintings, and my life because I wanted to help everyone, and I couldn't. Throughout my years of hearing their stories, it stressed me to the point of breaking. I realized that I must return to my art and find myself, even though I did not complete my art studies due to the financial burden. Instead, I focused on my art to find my true self.

ART ON THE ROAD

I participated in an art contest in Peru and was able to get a scholarship to become an arts and craft teacher at Cetpro Maria Auxiliadora. I studied jewelry designs at the Peruvian Institute of Jewelry and Art, including classes in Brazil. I had an amazing experience displaying my creations and showing the techniques I used on a Peruvian TV show. During all my adult life, I have been taking different courses and studying art techniques.

I moved to Puerto Rico and traveled to different towns doing local arts and crafts shows. Eventually, I moved to Wisconsin where I volunteered a couple of times at the local children's museum. I had a great opportunity to lead an art project there. The theme was "Peru," so I created a big painting featuring my home country and taught them all about it. During that week, children participated in filling in this painting using stencils, finger painting, and other techniques. More than one hundred children (including my lovely daughter) helped create this wonderful work of art which was exhibited at the Madison Children's Museum in 2007.

Soon after, I moved to Memphis, Tennessee and was able to donate paintings to be exhibited in some Tennessee towns.

In 2010, I went back to Peru and taught polymer clay and resin jewelry design workshops. I studied Peruvian stitch techniques to create wire crochet jewelry directly from Juan Pacheco, creator of the medium. Inspired by his monumental work, I implemented other variations to the same technique using different sizes of crochet hooks and different qualities and thicknesses of colored wires. I am now working to create a new mixed media wire crochet technique.

By 2012, I was back in the U.S. and settled down in Naperville, Illinois. I joined the Naperville Art League (NAL) in 2014 and have taught metal crochet workshops for more than four years. I've also exhibited my wire crochet creations at their gallery.

I was also honored to be selected for a show called "Women," at the nearby Aurora Museum. It was my first exhibit in an art museum, and I showed a range of wire crochet wearable art. It was humbling to meet women with such amazing talent. I'm also a member of the DuPage Art League (DUPAL) and Gallery 200 in West Chicago for the last three years (where I had a solo exhibit in 2017). I have won several merit awards from DUPAL and NAL. Last year, the Crochet Guild of America awarded me first place in the wearable art category.

In November of 2018 in Lima, I received an award from Gran Estrella de Plata in recognition of my metal crochet artwork. Juan Pacheco, creator of the Peruvian Stitch, acknowledged me as the only artist in the world using the technique in mixed media application. The next year, I received a bronze medal award in the

Fire Mountain Gems Metal Contest in the fashion accessories category.

SPIDER MOM

Every day, I wake up with the thought of creating something unique. Life is not easy. There are chronic health problems in my family, so I need me to be strong and keep working hard. I need to create every day. So I'm always looking at everything that surrounds me and influences my creativity. One of my creations is called "Everything is OK," and has two meanings if you turn it two different ways...just like life.

My past experience has truly made me the artist and the person, wife, and mother that I am today. I have learned that everyone can overcome obstacles in life if you don't give up. To be successful, we need to fail and to embrace our failure to be able to accept ourselves. We need to see the light in every storm that presents itself and to love what we do. For me, that means using my passion to bring smiles to people's faces.

I am a proud Latina of Peruvian heritage and want to always represent my country in my art, wherever I may be. Teaching Peruvian Stitch technique is one of my passions. I motivate students to create their own designs and I usually keep in contact with them after class ends. It gives me great joy to see their creative growth. People admire my ability to create different art pieces and transform their feelings and thoughts into unique art. My Latina friends continue to inspire me to be open to new ideas.

It is a challenge to balance being a mom and an artist but

being a mom is my priority. Between mixed media, wearable art, and jewelry design, my work takes a huge amount of time which is often spent at odd hours.

It is in the quiet of the night that I can feel the powerful energy emerging in the creation of my work. My family named me "The Spider Mom." People are often surprised when I tell them I always carry a spool of wire and a crochet hook in a small bag for when I am feeling inspired to work on a project. Each one begins with a simple idea and develops into something beyond my control.

My family is a great part of my inspiration and my creations are made with a lot of thought and countless hours of research, which I do while my kids are sleeping. Sometimes I work while waiting to pick them up at school, during weekend classes, doctor's appointment, etc. Sometimes a simple walk outdoors with my family can inspire a new theme. To use wire crochet technique, I design as many geometric shapes and abstract shapes as I need to create a unique, big, and amazing piece. I am always finding new ways to improve my technique.

Every day, I take pictures and videos of my work in progress for Instagram and Facebook and answer people's questions. It's fun when people guess what I'm doing because I give inspiration to my followers. I love to share with them and give them advice if they ask. I find it important to capture images of my work because each piece is different. If I see in my creation something that does not look right, I take it apart and start again. So I learn through my failures and I always remember my mistakes are my best teachers.

I love what I do and every thought that is put into my creations makes me feel great. LED wire crochet is my latest crazy idea. Although I have a couple of creations using LED, I am still researching. All my life, I have worked to be a unique creator. I hope my unique art pieces may inspire others to believe that they too can do it and have fun in the process. Whether you wear it or hang it in your home or office, my art not only brings beauty, but also happiness, peace, love, hope, etc. For me, it is also therapy and allows me to express my feelings. My dream is to someday create a large sculpture with wire and a big crochet hook. Right now though, I feel good creating smaller pieces with the technique and raising my kids. I feel blessed that God gives me the ability to create and a gift to share with everybody to give color and hope for their lives.

Thank you to my lovely husband, my kids, my mom, my family and friends who support me in someday making my dreams come true.

REFLECTION QUESTIONS

1. How do you bring creativity into your life?

2. When life gets stressful, what is your escape?

3. What did you do as a child that you still enjoy doing today?

BIOGRAPHY

Marita Valdizan is an internationally acclaimed, Peruvian, mixed media artist specializing in wire crochet and wearable art. Her roots are reflected in the wide palette of colors, textures, and materials she uses in her custom jewelry design and art. She tries to make every recipient of her art feel as unique as each original work.

Marita has awards from the DuPage Art League (DUPAL) and the Naperville Art

League (NAL). In 2018, she won first place in the wearable art category from the Crochet Guild of America and was awarded the Gran Estrella de Plata in Peru. In 2019, she was acknowledged as the world's only Peruvian Stitch artist in mixed media application. In 2019, she won a bronze medal in the Fire Mountain Gems Metal Contest, fashion accessories category.

She has also shown her art in Puerto Rico, Wisconsin, and Tennessee. Currently, her work is available at galleries in Aurora, Naperville, Wheaton, and West Chicago and online at Fine Art America.

Marita's values center around family, art, and giving back to her community. She teaches classes to adults and children in Spanish and English and has donated her artwork for local fundraisers. Find her on Instagram and Facebook.

Marita Valdizan
marita@waalay.com
Facebook: Marita Valdizan Arte

Beth Marmolejos

"From the moment I was born, I was blessed with a mission and purpose."

I was born in Santo Domingo, Dominican Republic. My parents were definitely not expecting me; my mom had had one ovary removed and my oldest siblings were 10-11 years older. So, I was a BIG surprise, especially when I arrived a month early!

When my older siblings were young, my father owned a gas station and we enjoyed a comfortable, upper-middle class lifestyle that included nannies, a nice car, a chauffeur, and lavish birthday parties. My father emigrated to New York, promising to bring us later. Then, when I was six months old, he surprised my mother with a divorce, leaving her with practically nothing. I never knew the privileged life of my siblings. With only a high school diploma, my mother became the sole provider for four children.

She was resilient and worked two jobs. She became an executive assistant to the president of a big corporation, Industria del Vidrio. She also became secretary to two Dominican presidents (Balaguer and Guzmán) and taught English and French in the evenings to blue collar workers who were trying to complete high school.

CONFIDENCE AND ME

From the moment I was born, I was blessed with a mission and purpose. My mother used to take me to work and I played in the accounting department with an old-fashioned adding machine. From that, I decided I was going to go to college and work in an office. I also learned to be comfortable around senior leaders, because my mother and I would lunch with the executive team. Interacting with them built my confidence and had a big impact on me. I even went on to earn an accounting degree and a master's degree in finance – with honors.

One of my mother's greatest legacies was her help to low-income students who could not afford textbooks. As an alternative, she would publish a pamphlet with lessons that they needed to study for her class. She also had me help her grade student exams with a "sample test" and always reminded me that her students were hard working, low income people. If they missed a point or two to pass, I needed to help them. This early experience taught me to help the less fortunate.

Another person who influenced me was my oldest sister, Natasha, whose goal was to keep me and David, my brother, busy. She paid for us to take swimming lessons, ballet, karate, painting, and more.

I loved ballet but martial arts became a passion. I loved the discipline, learning the moves and choreography, and the fact that my siblings and my cousin Edgar, with whom I was very close, also practiced with me. When I was seven years old and the only girl in my class, I trained with men and boys between 7-18 years old with our karate sensei, Rafaelito Medina. Sometimes he had me take over the class for a short time, and that experience made me feel strong and confident.

A pivotal moment occurred when my sister took my brother, my cousin, and me to a national karate competition without my mother's consent, and I won second place after defeating older, male opponents. I lost to an 18-year-old brown belt. At that moment, I realized that I was going to be a fighter... and that's what I have become!

THE VISION

I have experienced many unexplainable things. In seventh grade, I was treasurer of a boating trip that our teacher organized without the knowledge of the school principal. The night before, my sister Aida, who had moved to the U.S., dreamed that something was going to happen to my brother and me. She called my mother in the Dominican Republic to tell her about the nightmare. My mother thought of my trip and didn't let me go.

On that outing, seven classmates and the teacher drowned. It had been raining and water from the top of the mountain swept them away. My sister's vision saved my life because I would have been the first person to jump in since my best friend, who also had taken swimming lessons with me, was the first to go. She survived, but the girl she had invited to swim with her without telling our teacher, drowned. Had I been there, I probably would have joined her.

Another incredible experience was a tour to Italy and the Vatican where Pope John Paul II was holding a mass. I befriended two couples from Mexico who I met standing in line. With their help, I bypassed the guards without a ticket and touched the Pope's hand. It was quite a feat for someone who was not born Catholic but later converted, thanks to my godmother!

Similarly, I met famous evangelical pastor, Joel Osteen, and Father Emiliano Tardif, who was like a Pope in Latin America and used to stay in the U.S. at my godmother's house. Amazingly, both John Paul II and Father Emiliano were both canonized and to this day, I feel blessed, but also puzzled by how I met them both.

STUDYING – MY "SAFETY BLANKET"

I was an average student in elementary school, but in high school I resolved to get A's. My best friends were exceptional students and I studied hard to keep up with them and compete for the honor roll. I enjoyed studying, never missed school, and I realized that if I wanted to get top grades, I needed to study hard, be disciplined, and do my homework.

My mother, however, worried that I would fry my brain by studying too much. But I found that studies, homework, books, and classes were my safety blankets. Most high school students (including my children) find school boring. I, however, loved going to school and I kept engaged in class by taking notes, volunteering, and helping my teacher grade exams. My helpfulness was noticed by my calculus teacher in the Universidad

Nacional Pedro Henriquez Urena (UNPHU), who offered me an internship, and then a job, at a computer center. That job opened the door for my brother and me to qualify for a Visa that got us to the U.S. Raising my hand and serving others has helped me get promoted throughout my career.

IF YOU WANT SOMETHING, BE BOLD

When I was 13, my mother was secretary to the Dominican President, Salvador Guzmán. She invited me and some friends to visit her at the Presidential Palace. As the guide stopped to talk to someone, I had my friends take the elevator. We were resolved to meet the president. We found our way to his office and asked the guards if we could see him. They went to the generals, who were with the President, and told them about us.

The generals came out and asked how we got there. I replied that I was the daughter of Carmen Espinal, the president's assistant, and we came to meet him. We greeted the president, and he proudly showed us a picture of his wife and Pope John Paul II. Soft-spoken and very amicable, the president spoke to us for a few minutes. When I told my mother what had happened, she grinned at me and said she was proud of what I had done.

I also demonstrated perseverance when my high school principal banned graduation parties. We formed a committee to raise money for one with the help of our chemistry teacher. I was treasurer and collected money from my classmates every week.

I produced a concert with a famous band, "Los Hermanos Andrés," in a big auditorium. My classmates and I found companies to sponsor our graduation party with a band at an upscale hotel. I guess that proves that I never give up!

BE A MAGNET FOR CAREER OPPORTUNITIES

Wonder no more how to attract the best career opportunities. Build a reputation of integrity and commitment, and opportunities will find you, through senior leaders/mentors/sponsors who know your work and how committed you are to their success.

I am an executive advisor in the IT Account Management area at Anthem, the largest for-profit, managed care company in the Blue Cross Blue Shield association. I am also Chief of Staff of the Women's Inspire Network Associate Resource group and local lead of SOMOS Associate Resource Group.

That's just my day job. In addition, I am the vice president of the Prospanica New Jersey Chapter (formerly the National Society of Hispanic MBAs - NSHBMA) and chair of the Passaic County Workforce Development Board, among other positions. I have received awards from local, state, federal, corporate and non-profit organizations for my leadership and community work. I have managed to craft a professional life that fits my style, my passions, and goals. Through these commitments I have created career opportunities for myself and for those in my network.

I have had quite a career, beginning in the business world without a degreeat an entry-level position in the accounting department at Express Scripts (formerly known as Medco Health Solutions). While there, I got my undergraduate and graduate degrees, 80 percent of which were paid for by my employer as long as I earned a "B" or better in the class.

It took me more than ten years to complete my education. Meanwhile, I moved around the finance area into different roles and gained skills that helped me prepare for the role of controller/director of finance for a subsidiary that my company bought. It was valued at $2 billion when the president of our specialty division and the vice president of finance left the company due to disagreements with the parent company. Their departure allowed me to step up and help our senior leaders integrate the financial systems and develop consolidated reporting for them. I got promoted to a leadership position.

In 2013, I took a leap of faith and took a job at Empire BCBS in New York City under the leadership of a colleague from Medco, Brian Griffin, an amazing leader and sponsor. The best part of the move was my promotion six months later after leading a litigation project with the New York Department of Financial Services (NYDFS) that saved the company $1M.

Eighteen months later, I went to my former boss, now the president of Missouri BCBS, to ask for more work. Every couple of years, I get this itch to learn something new. He recommended me for the enterprise-level role as executive advisor in IT supporting the states of New York and Wisconsin. I enjoy this role because I function as a "fixer." By the time the problem gets to me, I need to re-assess it and pull together a team to solve it. I also love that my job allows me to align my passion for helping people in need through my non-profit work.

BEST PRACTICES TO STAY FOCUSED AND FIND OPPORTUNITIES

In addition to having faith in God, I have applied these practices to help me focus, get promoted, and avoid falling into the office politics trap:

- Remain calm and focus on what you are trying to achieve.
- Don't worry about things you cannot control.
- Surround yourself with positive people who help you stay on course.
- Treat people with respect and be a team player (I try to make everyone feel valued – it's the Latina in me!)
- Build/leverage your reputation to get better career opportunities in your organization.
- Be a can-do person; it's key to getting opportunities for senior roles.
- Be happy, positive, and knowledgeable; attract people who want to work with you.
- Find mentors and a good career coach who can provide guidance to navigate difficult situations at work. They have been a saving grace for me!

I hope my story shows what can be achieved through hard work and a positive attitude. I have risen through the ranks and now play a leadership role in many organizations. I also help Hispanic professionals, especially my Latina sisters, achieve success by opening doors and inspiring them. Most importantly, I am committed to ensuring that more people like me sit at the leadership table.

REFLECTION QUESTIONS

1. What best practices can you put in place to help you achieve more in your career?

2. Can you think of a time that you had to summon your confidence to get what you wanted?

3. Do you have some way to align your work, life, and values, such as your support of a non-profit or cause?

BIOGRAPHY

Beth Marmolejos is an Executive Advisor in IT Account Management at Anthem and a trusted partner for the New York and Wisconsin markets for IT functionality and services. She currently serves as Chief of Staff for the Women's Inspire Network Associate Resource and is the local lead for SOMOS, Anthem's Hispanic Associate Resources Group.

Beth has won numerous awards for her leadership in the community. These include recognition by the Passaic County Board of Chosen Freeholders during "National Women's History Month" in March 2019, a 2017 North Jersey Federal Credit Union Woman History-Maker Award, and Passaic County Salute of Champions for Disability 2017 Award.

She is committed to ensuring education and economic prosperity for all. Beth serves on the board of New Jersey Prospanica Chapter, Passaic County Advocacy and Abilities Committee, Passaic County 4Cs Board of Trustees, the American Association of University Women – Greater Wayne Area, and the Passaic County Workforce Investment Board.

Beth graduated with honors from Farleigh Dickinson University with an MBA in Finance and a B.S. in Accounting. She is married to her high school sweetheart, with two beautiful sons, one of whom is autistic and inspires her volunteer work. She also holds a black belt in Taekwondo.

Beth Marmolejos
marmolejosb@hotmail.com
(973) 689-4007

I AM A MIRACLE

Adriana Méndez Snowden

"Miracle Living is not taking control of your existence, but letting go of it and allowing yourself to exist at a higher level."

I used to love and self proclaim myself a warrior after many years living as a victim, I got tired and I decided I should be a warrior instead, little did I know, that was even more exhausting, so there I was, going through life as an eternal battle.

Because it's what I had to do
because 'that's life'
because no one will do it for you.

But I'm done, I've had enough
I don't want the universe to keep sending me fights
I don't want to proclaim victories and win any more battles

I'm done carrying a heavy shield and my sword ready to use it

I'm not a warrior, I am a miracle and I choose to flow
with life
with others
with the universe

with love
with compassion
with harmony
with detachment

I choose
to be grateful
to accept what I cannot change
and to have the courage to change the things I can
I choose

to be happy
to be resilient
to live in alignment

I'm a warrior no more

The greatest battle I won in my life
was when I completely surrendered to it.

I wrote this poem three years ago when I finally understood that I am a miracle, not a victim, nor a warrior, but a woman that accepts, surrenders, and flows with the reality she wants to create for herself, releasing all her superpowers to live a life full of miracles.

In my journey to my miracle, my identity shift led me to a life beyond my wildest dreams, filled with inner peace, love, and happiness, one day at a time. Everything started with one belief: all is possible with a commitment to personal growth.

As an *empath" and an "HSP" (highly sensitive person), I carry the gift of feeling other people's pain and struggles. I can read the energy of a broken heart, and cannot help but feel it too. It returns me to my old self, where I unconsciously chose to suffer in darkness, alone and pretending to be someone I wasn't, just to survive. Now my greatest wish and purpose comes from helping others transform their pain into miracles.

I want to convey a clear message of hope, resilience, love, faith, and believing in yourself and the miracles around and within you, no matter how hard and painful your life has been. You have the power to say, no more.

CRYING FOR HELP

In May of 2011, I was 33 years old, newly married to a wonderful man, and hitting rock bottom. My body, mind, and spirit were on the brink of self-destruction. I have been a functional alcoholic since I was 16. I left home when I was 18, so I mostly managed to hide it. My car accidents, visits to the hospital to pump my stomach, and getting arrested for public disturbances were all chalked up to being a young, free-spirited "party girl," when in reality I was a broken, depressed, alcoholic crying out for help.

At different points in my life I met with therapists and psychiatrists, attended spiritual retreats and shamanic rituals, always looking for answers, looking for love. Every little bit helped, but it didn't last, and I would return to my reckless and lonely life.

I know the root of my sadness, the exact moment my wings were torn. I was five years old when I was sexually abused, repeatedly. Unfortunately, we are not only victims once, because this becomes our identity. It happened again at 12 by a dance teacher and I didn't or "couldn't" say anything. The moment I started to drink, I discovered how I could numb my feelings and carry on, living *la vida loca* instead.

I met my first, "serious," boyfriend at 18. You know the one... not the one you marry but the one you will never forget because you gave him your virginity. My religious background taught that you were supposed to get married before having sex. Well, I broke that rule and felt I had betrayed God, in addition to feeling unworthy, ashamed and somehow guilty from my childhood trauma. Sadly, I had chosen the wrong guy, who only wanted "that.'"

I tried to kill myself on the day I found him in bed with another woman. I was saved by my mom but tried again when I found out he was getting married, and then again, and again. So after multiple suicide attempts, I saw our family doctor, who suggested I should meet this wonderful philanthropist man. He offered to take me and my brother out of my hometown in Mexico to get distance between myself and my past. I was deeply depressed, and we all thought it was for the best. What could go wrong? My brother and I would be together, living in an apartment with a fresh start, thanks to this kind gentleman. How lucky I was after all!

We departed a few weeks later in a private jet that was

waiting for us at the airport. I had never been on a plane before in my life, let alone a private one. My brother started work and university right away, while I was taken by the gentleman's assistant, chauffeur, and bodyguards to a high-end department store to get everything I needed. I bought hundreds of thousands of pesos in merchandise.

They were trying to change a hippy-ish, bohemian, small beach town girl into a sophisticated lady. That never worked, ha! But what they were also doing was grooming a naïve, 18-year-old that had never left her hometown to be the mistress of a gentleman twice her age who was being so kind to her family!

By the time I realized, I felt it was too late to leave. My brother was in one of the most prestigious private universities in México and we both had jobs and a new life. My phone lines were tapped and I had people follow me everywhere. Months later, I learned my "protector" belonged to one of the most powerful families in the country, the kind of power that appoints presidents. I was free to leave at any moment, but I had nowhere to go.

My family had dissolved in a matter of months. My parents got divorced after 22 years of a toxic and violent marriage and my mom remarried a man from England and left the country. My sister moved to another city and my brother moved to the U.S. My dad was starting a new family. So I stayed in my golden cage. My "boyfriend" was an alcoholic too, so we bonded over our addiction. My life consisted of luxury trips to Europe, yachts, private jet rides, prestigious Michelin restaurants and shopping sprees, but I remained sad, depressed, drunk, and ashamed.

NEW LIFE BACK HOME

It took eight years for me to gather the courage to leave. I returned to my hometown with nothing. I just wanted to be free, and now I was free, and broke. I went home to an empty house, the house I grew up in, and started work at a cell phone company. A few years went by where I was just surviving. All I cared about was having money to support myself and my drinking. I wanted to have fun, and I was careless. I got involved with all kinds of drug dealers and dreamt of being a mafia cartel queen myself. I was hungry for power and tired of being subjected to a man's will all my life. I tried, but thank God I got out.

Instead, I applied for a job in sales. My town is one of the most popular tourist destinations for Americans and Canadians and all I needed was to speak English, which I did. I loved my fast-paced, fun, highly paid job. The best thing of all was that my co-workers were all foreigners. They didn't know my past, so they didn't judge me like the locals did.

A few years later, I met the love of my life, the actual ONE. I knew it the moment I laid eyes on him. He was a British-Canadian, kind-hearted man. We both had partners back then, but we did what we needed to do to be together. We married in 2011, and about a month after our wedding, everything appeared to be great between us, except that it wasn't. I had hit rock bottom with my drinking. I was 33 years old and tired of living a double life and trying to hide my "problem." I had to admit my life was out of control or I wouldn't survive. This was hard because to the world our lives looked perfect. We had highly paid jobs, we were living in a luxury beach condo, and driving luxury sports cars. But internally, I was going through hell, just a month after our dream wedding. It looked like a fairy tale, but we were falling apart.

Finally, I asked for help and that's when my recovery journey began. After a year and a half of sobriety, my fairy tale came true when we had our son, the most beautiful little prince. We thought we would live happily ever after.

FINDING MIRACLES

Then the universe gave us a "present" that we didn't recognize as a gift. In 2015, we suddenly had to leave Mexico. It was a deep bottom for us. We were unprepared, having lost our savings. We came to England, and thanks to the support of my husband's family, we were able to start over, in an even better way than I expected.

After sending out dozens of CVs, having interviews and not being hired, I interviewed for a position for a Spanish-speaking sales representative, which I thought was a sure thing. I didn't get it!

After recovering from that disappointment, I took a part-time job in a fish and chips shop offered to me by my friends who owned it. Later, I came to realize this was part of the gift from the universe that had been looking after me all along. I realized I had been applying for jobs with feelings of desperation, fear, scarcity, and sadness for losing time with my little boy. So it's not what you say or do that determines your fate, but the vibrations that you send out to the universe. By taking that part-time job, I could be with my son and I could follow my dream and fulfill a mission to become a mentor, an international speaker, and a writer. So I immersed myself fully in my education. Living with my in-laws allowed me to invest time and money in self-development courses, coaching programs, seminars, books, etc.

So while I washed dishes and pans in the back of the shop, I was visualizing myself talking to a beautiful audience. I could see myself writing books and helping people. I could see the version of myself I wanted to become.

A few months later, I got my first speaking engagement in Amsterdam, then in Liverpool, England, Puerto Vallarta, México, and Barcelona, Spain. I ran transformational retreats and mentored people one-on-one and in groups. I published a couple of books. And it all started when I believed and understood I was a miracle and my purpose was to serve and share with others how to shift their identity into the ones they want, where they see the life they've only imagined, full of miracles.

I created Miracle Mindset Academy to be who I am today, through developing soul-awareness, responsibility, and commitment to my growth. By accepting the things I cannot change and changing the ones I can, I have the clarity to use the Law of Attraction in my favor and understand that "Miracle Living" is not taking control of your existence, but letting go of it and allowing yourself to exist at a higher level.

REFLECTION QUESTIONS

1. What miracles have occurred in your life that you did not recognize at the time?

2. What do you do when you encounter a situation you must escape?

3. What kind of vibrations do you send to the universe? What can you do to make them more positive?

BIOGRAPHY

Adriana Méndez Snowden is a transformational leader and author who fulfills her purpose in helping others by speaking internationally and in her books. She is the author of Happiness through Resilience, a topic she considers vital to achieving success, as well as two books of poetry, *Mujer Onírica* (first edition) and *Mujer Onírica, the before and after.* The latter book reflects Adriana's internal transformation, 20 years after struggling with alcoholism and childhood wounds. She now lives a miraculous life.

Adriana's mission is to empower women and men through coaching, online seminars, books, conferences and international transformational retreats. Not only is she committed to her purpose from her own development and preparation, but also to overcoming adversity throughout her life. She defines success as living a full and happy life on your own terms and achieving a conscious alignment with the universe.

Originally from Puerto Vallarta, Mexico, where she lived most of her life, Adriana recently moved to England with her husband and little son. Although a difficult change, it has driven and motivated her to develop her program and next book, *Miracle Mindset: 12 Steps to Soul Recovery.*

Adriana Méndez Snowden
contact@adrianamendezsnowden.com
+44 742 8990790

Alicia Ponce-Nuñez

"They wanted to bury us. They didn't know we were seeds."

As an architect, I believe that every human being should have access to clean air and water, sunlight, a breeze, and a cozy corner to call their own. Architecture has the power to provide all of that through forms, patterns, and colors. With technology rapidly evolving, we have the ability to do things like create materials that store solar energy instead of relying on fossil fuels to heat or cool a building. We can also use alternative, environmentally friendly materials in lieu of plastics that end up in landfills and ultimately pollute our oceans. Now more than ever, I believe in what I do. Humanity is facing a global climate crisis and we have the tools and resources to make it better for our immediate future and generations to come.

Starting a business was never on the radar for me but now I am an entrepreneur on a mission. When I think about it, my destiny as an architect was a long time in coming.

A BORN ARCHITECT

When I was seven years old, I knew that I wanted to be an architect. I have always considered myself a very inquisitive person and my love for art and architecture fed my curiosity to learn more about how things were made and explore the many different ways to bring comfort and joy to a person in their space.

As a child, I had a pen pal who happened to be my great-uncle Chencho. He was a priest who lived in Rome. In my letters, I would ask him to describe the buildings to me in every detail. He always described them as very, very old. I yearned to know more and he talked to me about the historic architecture. These letters may have been the seeds that were planted in me to dream of one day studying in Europe.

I am eternally thankful to my parents and my wonderful family role models. To this very day, I hear my mother in one ear saying, "Soar as high as you want. You can do anything!" In the other ear, I hear my father telling me, "I didn't think you would turn out so smart!" He supported my every idea, even if he didn't quite get it.

Growing up, I also felt a strong connection with nature. My parents would drive me and my siblings to the state of Michoacán in Mexico to visit our family. I didn't realize it then but those summers gave me the freedom to enjoy nature up close. I can close my eyes anytime and visualize the winding roads through the green mountains, the fields of sugarcane, the fisherman sailing on Lake Pátzcuaro, and of course, the monarch butterflies floating above my head. In 1981, we actually lived there for one year. I remember staying in bright colorful adobe houses and being completely immersed in beautiful landscapes of trees and calming streams.

When we returned to Illinois, we moved to Summit, just 20 minutes southwest of downtown Chicago. Back then, it was predominantly a Polish-American neighborhood and sometimes Mexican families in the park with their children received unfriendly remarks.

I was enrolled in school and I had to re-learn English at the age of eight. To my horror, the ESL teacher would often hit us and make me cry by giving me *coscorroneson* my head for moving my lips while silently reading. The only one in the school that was one of "us"-- a Mexican with a dark complexion like me-- was such a witch. Believe me when I say that I learned as quickly as I could and was in the honor roll every year after that.

It is the firm belief in oneself and the willingness to step into the unknown that will lead you to your chosen path. So, if you watch and listen closely, the doors will open. I even look for windows. In high school, I was a model student and athlete and was sure I was on the right path to becoming an architect. When it came time to apply for college, in the days before Google and the world wide web, I took the next step and sat down with my counselor to talk about schools, specifically, the University of Illinois at Urbana-Champaign. The school had a greatreputation for architecture majors, and most importantly, it had a study abroad program in Versailles, France.

To my big surprise, the conversation with the counselor was not what I expected. I cannot even remember his name, but I remember sitting in his office, looking to him as a trusted advisor, to talk about my application to my first choice school. Instead, he put the local community college application in front of me and said, "Why don't you start here and in two years you can transfer."

I wasn't upset that he was handing me this application; I was upset that he wouldn't even let me try even though I had the grades to prove that I could succeed there. I walked away feeling confused and unsupported. I wanted to attend the University of Illinois very badly, but he told me that the school would be too challenging for me.

Lucky for me, Mr. Johnson was in my world. He was my English teacher and saving grace who helped me through the whole college application process and wrote an amazing letter of recommendation. Because of his support, I was accepted into the University of Illinois' Architecture school, studied in Versailles, and traveled throughout Europe while there.

The experience with the counselor was one of many that would remind me of the old Mexican proverb, "They wanted to bury us. They didn't know we were seeds." I knew I was the seed and also that my gender nor my ethnicity would be a roadblock to my dreams. Instead, they were the building blocks to endless possibilities. This belief was not always clear to me but it was always living inside of me. I know this because with every setback or disappointment I have faced, I was being prepared for something much bigger. In the long run, the way a person responds to difficult times is what matters most. When life throws you rotten tomatoes, make compost!

LEED DESIGNER

In the summer of 2006, I was working in a small boutique firm that was building "McMansions" inthe Bucktown neighborhood of Chicago. I was hired as their green building and LEED design specialist, which was something that I had developed a passion for over the past ten years and had longed to do at my past three employers. LEED stands for Leadership in Energy and Environmental Design and it is an internationally recognized building rating system which certifies buildings that have been designed to be healthy, highly efficient, and sustainable for the environment. In my time at the firm, there was only one client who ever inquired about LEED.

Through my years of independent research, I was ready to do some very transformative work; I just needed an opportunity. Unfortunately, all I ever did was prepare drawings for porch repairs to bring buildings up to code while working at the small firm. Although it was work, it was not the type of work I was promised, nor the type that inspired me to go to work every day and call myself an architect.

I was there for one year when I was called into my supervisor's office. To my surprise, I was laid off. Their aspiring green building design specialist was kicked to the curb just like that! I honestly had no words for what I was feeling. I was hurt, but looking back on it now, it was the timely kick in the pants I needed. Little did I know that the residential McMansion bubble was about to burst across the nation.

I remember going to my desk to gather my things. I said

goodbye to my co-workers who had become my friends. One of them in particular, who I still keep in touch with, said to me with conviction, "Alicia, don't worry. And remember, anything is possible!"

With that, like a light bulb turning on over my head, I remembered the single client that came into the office to talk about LEED! I grabbed my bag, my coat, and his contact information. When I got home, I laid on my bed and stared at the ceiling for a long time, asking myself if I should call the number. I basically had to get myself pepped up for the call. I didn't have a plan. All I had was a strong desire to build green buildings. I had no kids and I was single. The only responsibility I had was me and my mortgage. So, with that, I made the call. Within four weeks, I had rented my condo on Michigan Avenue, sold my car, and moved into my aunt's living room!

I founded my business, APMonarch, on June 4th in 2007. That fall, I was traveling to New Orleans as the lead designer and sustainability consultant for my first, mid-rise, multi-family condominium. I was meeting with the council members of the city of New Orleans to talk to them about the revitalization of the city through sustainable design and high-performance buildings. I also had secured a couple of more contracts in Chicago and started teaching sustainability at Columbia College. I was living the dream!

Then, the housing market finally crashed in 2008, putting a complete halt to my projects and my fat paychecks. This setback taught me not to put all my eggs in one basket. Luckily, I was still living in my aunt's living room and was still single with no kids.

LATINA ARCHITECT

Long gone are the days of living with my aunt and hearing her tell me I was building character. Now, I am living on cloud nine with my husband and kids. Cesar and I met soon after I established APMonarch. Since the beginning, he has unconditionally supported my often unpredictable journey as an entrepreneur and architect. He is my Zen, and without him, I would not be able to soar as high and in as many directions as I do.

The year 2019 marked my twelfth year as a Latina entrepreneur who focuses on sustainability and resilient architecture. It is something that I wholeheartedly believe in and love doing.

Being a Latina in a white male-dominated industry has its share of experiences, from meeting lifelong mentors who give you wings, to disappointingly being caught in #metoo moments. Either way, I take these experiences and use them as building blocks to a chosen path.

I am one of only 20 percent of female licensed architects and only one percent Latina architects nationwide. The numbers get astoundingly smaller when you look at the number of female Latina architects who own a business! This motivates me to say "yes" to as many invitations from school career days to larger business professional settings. I'm here to answer as many questions that come my way to help guide the younger generation.

Twelve years in business have given me the absolute joy of

working with people both locally and internationally who are making a difference in the world and continue to build a healthier place for our children like the one I was able to enjoy as a child. Just as the monarch butterfly fearlessly and resiliently travels across borders, I am ready to make a bigger impact.

REFLECTION QUESTIONS

1. What is stopping you from getting what you want?

2. What are you most grateful for?

3. When you fail, (because you will) how will you turn those failures into valuable building blocks for your chosen path?

BIOGRAPHY

Alicia Ponce-Nuñez is the Founder and Principal of APMonarch, an architecture and design firm with a passion for sustainability. She founded the company in 2007, and has since completed numerous LEED and Living Building Challenge-certified projects. Her diverse portfolio includes such notable clients as The Field Museum, Midway International Airport, University of Chicago, and the Exelon Corporation.

She was the primary sustainability consultant for the University of Chicago's Keller Center - Harris School of Public Policy, which pursued many design firsts, inspired by the school's ethos of positive social change. Keller Center will be the first LEED Platinum building on campus and among the first in higher education to earn the rigorous Materials Petal Certification of the Living Building Challenge.

Her reputation secured APMonarch's role as the sustainability architect and direct protégé to Santiago Calatrava and his firm's design proposal for the O'Hare International Airport Global Terminal. An alumnus of the University of Illinois at Urbana-Champaign, Alicia is proud to be among the 20 percent of licensed female architects in the U.S. and among the one percent who are Latina.

Alicia Ponce has also made a name for herself as an actor, participating in riveting stage productions in Bogotá, Colombia.

Alicia Ponce-Nuñez
aponce@apmonarch.com
LinkedIn: /aliciaponce-apmonarch

171

Karina Mejía

"There will always be a flower growing from the impossible,
which will give us power to move forward."

The idea to work with marginalized families came from my own life story. I did not choose to work with families; they chose me!

I am Peruvian. I was born in Lima, in a neighborhood called Callao, on the street of Ramón Castilla. I lived there until I was ten, and then moved to Ramón Castilla after my parents divorced. Ramón Castilla was a neighborhood just outside the city, where homes were cheaper than in the rest of Callao.

For the next six years, we lived in a shack in the Angamos neighborhood in the Ventanilla district of Lima. I dreamed of becoming a dancer. After school, I would go play, but I had to return before six o'clock at night because if my mom caught me on the street she would ground me.

BORN AGAIN

One day, I was cleaning the floors of my house when my hand got caught in a electrical light connection. In a panic, I tried to grab a broomstick but couldn't reach. If it wasn't for my screams, which alerted my neighbor, "El Charapo," I could have died. He pulled me out of the current by my hair and turned off the light with a stick. In that instant, I felt that I was born again. I was sore all over and my fingers were burned from the electricity. But I was born again.

I remember an unusual force that ran through my veins, that force that Latina women are born and reborn with several times in life. We are warrior women, and we say to ourselves, "I am fine," because we know that in our path there will always be a flower growing from the impossible, which will give us power to move forward.

As the daughter of divorced parents and a single working mother, I was always the target of discrimination and teasing. However, at 14 years of age, it was already clear that nothing would stop me in life. My mother tried to make me a Quinceañera celebration, however I told her not to worry about that party; it was not important to me. I promised her that one day I would buy her a house and she wouldn't see her shack anymore. However, mom never asked me for anything; she only said that we had to be grateful for having a place to live.

A few years ago, I returned to my childhood neighborhood and looked for my friends from the past, but they were gone. I did not find the Los Charapos family, who received that name because they were all from the jungle. Ardilosa, a woman who used to sleep with married men, had died. Doña Juana, who used to bathe outside her house with a hose, had moved cities. José Luis, el Loco, was now a family man and worked as a garbage collector. These and other characters are part of the cast of my theatrical life.

My mother is a very beautiful woman with a very noble heart, who couldn't finish high school and always wanted me to accomplish more than her. I am who I am today thanks to her ideals, wise advice, and guidance. This led her to look for an opportunity to immigrate to Mexico, which made a tremendous impact on me. When I was 16, we moved to a world that responds to a different culture and set of rules. Every immigrant feels marginalized after seeing known things disappear and having to respond to so many new situations. These experiences led me to be seen as different and therefore able to relate well to marginalized families.

DAUGHTER OF MEXICO

Living in Mexico, I decided to look for a university that offered scholarships to foreign students. My years at Universidad del Noreste in Tamaulipas were filled with learning, from my observations on the street, in the classrooms, and what I read at the library, late into the night. Most of the students were from very wealthy families. There were only five or six in the whole university who came from working class families. I was the only Peruvian who had a rare accent and worked in a restaurant cleaning floors to pay for my studies and buy books. Perhaps many wondered what this young girl was doing among them in the university. It didn't take long for us to get used to each other.

In spite of how hard this time was for me, my desire for

self-improvement and love for education and psychology never died. I wanted to be a great professional and be able to help other people get ahead. I regarded this stage of life as a new path full of beautiful flowers to help others, so that I could prove that there are flowers in everyone's path.

While in college, I joined a Christian youth group sponsored by the Catholic Church. They invited me to join the ministry of music, "Salt and Light of the Earth." I must confess that they were the best years of my youth. There, I met my friends and we traveled to different small towns to work with young people, children, and their families, sharing the word of God and bringing them hope and some food to lessen their burdens.

During a group activity, I travelled to Mexico City, to the Basilica of Our Lady of Guadalupe. There I lived an extraordinary experience which was difficult to talk about because my heart was racing. I couldn't believe that on the day of my visit, Most Holy Mary of Guadalupe would receive me at her home and adopt me as her Mexican daughter. She gave me the confidence that I was in the land of bliss and progress and that I would never feel out of my homeland because Mexico was mine. That is how I stopped feeling like a foreigner in Mexican lands, and I made the commitment to help my people and pay back to my beloved Mexico a little for the opportunities it had given me.

After several weeks of interacting with my college classmates, I noticed how there were some who were only there until they found a rich husband to solve their problems. Others were there because they made a commitment to their parents to pursue a professional degree, and two others wanted to be the best teachers they could because they came from families filled with teachers. Back then, there was no technology that would let us isolate ourselves from others. We were forced to communicate with each other. We saw each other passing to and from class, and I became friends with one of my classmates. Her house was a living library, and she was very good at studying and presenting in class. Thanks to her, I learned new study habits and experienced a home library like no other. Her mother was a school teacher and her father was a music teacher. Whenever we arrived at her house, her mother had already fixed me a plate of hot food. I don't know if it was because I looked very skinny or because my friend told her about the sacrifices I was making to study at the University.

I also remember a young teacher who taught psychology with a lot of passion. She gave me the wise advice to study the discipline if I wanted to help the people around me. However, the readings she shared from Freud's books and the experiments of behaviorists, like B.F. Skinner, made no sense when applied to understanding the people around me. I studied philosophy and social anthropology in the search to find meaning and understand it. And little by little, I understood that the individual was more than his "psyche."

It's these little experiences that shape our character and how we code what happens around us. That is why the idea that "one chooses" a profession is questionable. As I write these notes, I am appreciating how the path presented itself to me. Inclinations are not isolated ideas; they are the exchange of our experiences with the circumstances. Some take advantage of them, but others decline the invitation.

PATH TO PSYCHOLOGY

That was how a teacher discovered my talent for helping and teaching. She took me to a very prestigious school in the city where they were searching for a teacher with my qualifications, and they hired me. In that institution, I learned a lot in daily practice, however I felt that I needed something else to be able to help each of my students. And that's where I got the opportunity to study a master's degree in family and couple's psychotherapy. It was that training that completed my work. Now I not only help my students, but also their families.

Psychotherapist training is not like training in other disciplines. A significant number of professions are not actively engaged in relationship with the public, nor does their professional success depend on therapeutic collaboration. A chemist, physicist, mathematician, or biologist can practice his profession without contact with the public. However, other professions depend on exchange with people, and cannot exist without people. The physical/mental health and psychotherapy professions are nothing without people. Hence, it's a valuable skill to be able to socialize with different groups in different situations. So that is why I have developed an interest in working with vulnerable families and children with difficult educational contexts, to help them discover new opportunities.

Through the years, I have realized that one of the main

ingredients to achieving success is helping others. I had been helping only a small group of families, children, and adolescents. If I wanted to help a larger group, I had to do something to impact the way people think. So five years ago, I decided to start writing part of the legacy I will leave to my four children. I founded the Ifam Tamaulipeco Family Institute, which is composed of a group of professionals in the field of mental, family, and educational health, whose main focus is training professionals in systemic family therapy. We offer psychologists, teachers, social workers, lawyers, and any professional who works directly with families, the tools and professional development they need to work with couples, children, and adolescents. The professionals of the Tamaulipeco Family Institute perform individual, family, and couples psychotherapy, creating contexts in which people can solve their interpersonal problems. Only practice and experiences with people led me to combine part of my teachings and my own life story to become an agent of change in my community and to be useful in my environment.

Two years ago, I was able to fulfill another dream by creating the "Building a New Woman" program, which has the sole objective of helping women share their life story and create an opportunity to make changes and transform their lives forever. The name is fitting because I learned to define myself and build myself into the woman I wanted to become. Other women can too. They just need to have the resources to be able to transform themselves.

Eight months ago, I was diagnosed with two thyroid

tumors. Over several terrible months, I went from doctor to doctor, hearing the word "cancer" presented as a very probable outcome. I underwent nuclear radiation tests and had to stay away from my children. They could only look at me from the door, but they couldn't hug me. One day my son, Jean Marco, left me a letter under the door with a flower that said in my path there will always be a flower. And so it is with life. When things look gloomy, I realize I can always get ahead and never lose sight of the true value of life.

All women are warriors by nature. Like many in our Latino community, we rise up a thousand times, illuminating everything around us, achieving the incredible, and weaving a support network so that more women discover our powerful strength and transform their lives.

REFLECTION QUESTIONS

1. What are the flowers in the path of your life that allow you to keep going?

2. How do you define yourself? Do you seek transformation?

3. Have you ever had an experience where you felt "born again?"

BIOGRAPHY

Karina Mejia was born in Lima, Peru but has lived in Matamoros, Tamaulipas Mexico for 22 years. Her passion is to activate the resources of families, couples, children, and adolescents in an agile and creative way to dissolve conflicts and create contexts in which people can resolve their personal problems. She is currently the director and founder of the Tamaulipeco Family Institute (Infam) in Mexico, which works primarily with marginalized families.

Karina is the mother of four beautiful sons and the wife of a man who loves her and supports her growth every day. She has served as a teacher since 1999 and as a family therapist and university professor since 2006. She became a licensed teacher in 2002 and obtained a master's degree in systemic family therapy from North American University in 2016. In 2012, she finished her PhD in Teaching Methodology from the Mexican Institute of Pedagogy.

Karina is a member of the National Association for the Education of Young Children (NAEYC) and a board member of the southern Texas chapter of the organization. She has appeared at various conferences and forums at the local, state, national and international levels in the United States, Chile, and Peru.

Karina Mejía
karinatf@infam.com.mx
956.734.4638

Lizbeth Ramirez

"Create lofty goals. Then when you face obstacles and failure, your goals will become your motivation to never give up."

I believe that the timing of circumstances always has a reason, even if we don't understand why something is happening in our lives at a certain moment.

Change has been a constant in my life, and I have learned to embrace it. One of the most pivotal changes was my family's move from our small and vibrant, Spanish-speaking town in the central-western part of Mexico. It was a small village with warm weather, where the beautiful, cultural sounds of Mariachi music could be heard year around. But in 1993, we made the journey to the bustling city of Chicago.

NEW CITY, NEW CHALLENGES

As a third grader, I struggled to understand why my parents believed it would be better for our family to move to a crowded, tiny apartment in a big American city that was known for its frigid temperatures and inclement weather than to stay in our village. Then, I realized that the people in this new city did not understand my native language. However, it was not very long before I, too, was speaking their language like I had been living in Chicago my entire life. I was accepting change.

After a few years, I learned to love this foreign place, that once felt so far from my tiny village, because Chicago was becoming my new home. As I continued my education in high school, I grew to learn that change is an inevitable part of life. Change brings the excitement of new places, new people, and new horizons.

To be candid, my excitement for my new home and community was mixed with intense moments of fear. I feared that as an immigrant, my contemporaries would place me in a box and label me in ways that I did not understand, and they did. I became stereotyped as the Latina, the undocumented, the Spanish speaker, and many of them assumed I would never make it to college.

Luckily, I was relieved from my fear at the age of 14 because that was the year I received my U.S. residency. Then, in my junior year of high school, I became a U.S. citizen. As I look back on that period of my life, I know that my acquisition of citizenship was possible because my father received his own residency in 1985, when President Ronald Reagan's administration began an amnesty program for undocumented immigrants living in the United States.

While I initially associated change with challenge as a little girl, in high school I learned that change also brought good things into my life. When I was eight years old, my parents decided to change my life forever by moving my family to Chicago. Now it was my turn to make a change. This change was related to their cultural beliefs that I should marry a nice man while still young and raise a family.

But I was a determined teenager, and I fought for what I believed in. I wanted to pursue a college education. My father thought he was being opened-minded by allowing me to attend a community college. It was then that I realized my biggest struggle would be with my own parents. At the age of 18, without their permission, I made my first adult decision to leave home and go away to attend college. As I arrived at the University of Illinois at Urbana-Champaign campus, I was mesmerized by what would be my new home for the next four years.

As an international studies major, I was required to study abroad as part of the curriculum, which became the reason I chose that career path. With international studies I had the opportunity to focus on a field, an area, and a language. I chose political science, Latin America, and Spanish. I was hungry for knowledge and to experience this world we live in.

In the fall semester of my junior year in college, I embarked on a journey to "study abroad" in the city where I was born--Guadalajara, Jalisco-- to fulfill my semester abroad. I had decided on Mexico as a negotiation strategy with my father, who was not thrilled with my first choice of going to Brazil. When I arrived in Mexico, I thought I knew it all, but little did I know I knew nothing about the country for which I felt the greatest admiration and love. After one semester abroad, I had visited more than ten cities and six of the 32 states of the Republic of Mexico. I experience Independence Day in Mexico City, Day of the Dead in Michoacán, and visited multiple small towns known as "Los Pueblos Mágicos." This was just the beginning of my love for travel.

RAISED EXPECTATIONS

My college years flew by, and in May 2007, I graduated and became the first member of my immediate family to earn a college degree. Furthermore, I was the first woman in my family to get an education beyond high school. This was a significant departure from what had been the traditional role of women in my family. My parents quickly realized that my independence wasn't a problem; it was a strength. I managed to successfully graduate and earn my bachelor's degree, study abroad, and find a job to build my future.

This was a pivotal moment for my family. It created a real change in their mindset that having an educated daughter was not a bad thing. Their aspirations and expectations for my little sister were now higher. There was no doubt that my younger sister was now expected to go to college and graduate. My parents had begun to accept change in their cultural beliefs.

Shortly after graduation, I started my first full-time job working in state government, and to really shake things up in my life, I took on a political role within the Democratic Party. Talk about a fish out of water. Expectations of me were at an all-time low as I encountered comments such as "Latinos don't last in this job" and "you will probably only stay here for two years."

Despite this "warm welcome," I worked for the Illinois House of Representatives for seven years. I learned the ins and outs of the legislative process and developed relationships with elected officials from both sides of the aisle. I became the go-to person to pass legislation. As a political operative, I won every single election that I managed or volunteered to help. I don't know if it was a record, but for this Latina, it was an accomplishment! My position taught me to understand different points of view and empathize with individuals who came from different communities than mine. It also gave me insight into the stereotypes and labels I had received as an immigrant. For those reasons, I channeled my work ethic into breaking the stereotypes. I took it as a challenge, professionally and personally.

When I began my career in government, I was required to work long hours, which only inspired me to take a "real vacation," which meant that I wasn't satisfied with solely traveling to Mexico or nearby states. I wanted to see the world. At that time, having a cell phone was a luxury and having one abroad was a very expensive option. Therefore, while abroad, I could not take work calls. Lucky me! I was liberated!

When I was 24, I decided to go backpacking through Europe. As a new traveler, I convinced my two childhood friends to travel with me. This was my first trip away from my norm, not to Mexico, and outside of the United States. For 20 full days, I visited two countries, stayed in five cities and received a lifetime of experiences that opened my eyes and curiosity to exploring my world. What a difference for a young girl who once felt out of place in her own community. The world was now mine. Today, I can say without any regret that I have traveled to approximately 20 countries and numerous cities.

Professionally, I was ready to move on to bigger challenges. I had worked in government for seven highly successful years.

Given my experience, I decided to pursue work in the private sector. I chose to build on my legislative success and became an in-house corporate lobbyist. At the age of 29, I joined a top-notch lobbying team as the youngest lobbyist and only Latina. Within two years, our team was successful in ushering through the passage of one of the most substantial pieces of legislation that fundamentally changed our company's industry in the State of Illinois.

Because of my work and to my surprise, I was nominated and won "Best In-House Lobbyist" by a highly political news publication in Springfield. My work was publicly validated.

The transition from government service to the corporate sector brought significant change in my life. I had proven myself to others, but also to myself. I was no longer the Latina lobbyist, the young lobbyist, or the female lobbyist. I was no longer the undocumented girl. I was no longer the Mexican girl with preconceived family "traditions" to follow. I was now simply Lizbeth. It was me. It was an empowering moment for me.

FROM STRUGGLE TO SUCCESS

I have been able to channel my adversity into success and I am proud to be an immigrant who struggled through school, cultural changes, making friends, and adapting to continuous changing environments to achieve what I have so far in life. Through these experiences, I have learned that no one can define who I am and what I want to do. If I had allowed people to define me, I would not be where I am today.

My professional career in government has created a passion for law in my heart. I have seen firsthand how policy can affect the lives of people. I want to have a more active role in taking policy ideas and making them into law. I want to use this opportunity to help other young Latinas like myself who may also being stereotyped because of their background, their accent, their socioeconomic status, their race, or gender. I hope to inspire these young women and give them the chance to see someone that they can relate to with a background like their own. I want them to know that they can achieve all that seems impossible.

It was through my determination that I have tackled every obstacle that comes my way with a positive attitude, I have transformed myself in many ways. I believe we should create lofty goals. Then when you face obstacles and failure, your goals will become your motivation to never give up, even when no one else believes you can achieve them.

Even though there were times when I felt alone in my battles, I know that I didn't get here all by myself. There are many who served as my support system to lean on during those difficult periods in my journey. As I look back, it wasn't only my persistence, curiosity, and hunger for knowledge that helped me move forward, embrace change, and breakthrough all the challenges I have faced. It was my parents who instilled a sense of pride in me and were there at 12 a.m. waiting to cook for me after working long campaign days and drove hours to drop off documents I needed for work. They did my laundry so I could sleep, accommodated family events to fit my work schedule, and where always there, no matter what, waiting to let me know that tomorrow was another day to conquer my challenges.

REFLECTION QUESTIONS

1. What forces contribute to the way you define yourself? (You, friends, family, society, etc.)

2. What lofty goals have you set for yourself?

3. What stereotypes have you experienced and what have you done to break them?

BIOGRAPHY

In a classic immigrant story, Lizbeth Ramirez immigrated to Chicago from Guadalajara, Mexico in 1993. Her early years in Mexico shaped her desire to give back, which is evident in both her public and private life.

Lizbeth studied political science at the University of Illinois Urbana-Champaign and became a program specialist for the Democratic Party. She worked with Democratic legislators to develop and implement legislation. She engaged community organizations, civic groups, and political leaders on issues ranging from education to redistricting. She also worked with Democratic party candidates on campaigns and winning strategies.

In 2016, Lizbeth joined an in-house corporate lobbying team in Springfield and worked to pass legislation that put Illinois at the forefront of investing in renewable energy and creating jobs. That year, she was named "best in-house lobbyist" by Capitol Fax.

Lizbeth currently serves as an in-house lobbyist in Chicago and Cook County for an energy company, working with elected officials on initiatives relevant to the company. She also volunteers with organizations that promote women's advancement and leadership, such as Leadership Illinois, and on the boards of the Rauner Family YMCA and the Illinois Legislative Latino Caucus Foundation.

Lizbeth Ramirez
Lgramire@gmail.com
@Traveler.Foodie.Lizbeth

Adriana Hernández Martínez

"Use all your positivity and belief in yourself to forge your own success."

My life in Mexico and Europe has not been a Cinderella story or a Barbara Cartland novel. My story is more Mexican: nice and spicy, flavored with a little struggle and lightly seasoned with perseverance and a pinch of salt (for good luck!)

I am Adriana Hernández Martínez and I am Mexican. I left my country with my son, Lalo, in my arms and 26 years of my life in two suitcases. I left behind everything I knew and loved and left my comfort zone in search of the unknown. I went to the other side of the world and arrived in The Netherlands in 1996. Now, 23 years later, I have fully assimilated into this beautiful country and I'm Dutch. It feels very good. When I decided to write this chapter, I did it because I would have loved to have had a book like this in the past to teach me that I am not alone in coping with a move to a new country, and to inspire and encourage me to keep moving forward.

Like you, I had many doubts and moments of despair during my move, but I have always been certain that everything would be fine. I have always trusted myself and never given up. And although I sometimes still take a step backwards, it's only in order to move forward again.

I am currently a Dutch politician for the 50PLUS party. I want to help prevent and solve the problems generated by the aging population in the Netherlands and Europe. I hold several political positions. I am Councilor of the City of 's-Hertogenbosch and a board member of the Water Council Aa and Maas. The Maas is a river that crosses Holland from east to west, dividing the country in two parts. I am also a staff member of the 50PLUS parliamentary faction in the European Parliament.

How does it feel to hold these honors? Fantastic! I remember the night of the election, when I saw the results that we had won. We all embraced and congratulated each other. After many years of hard work, we were finally there! The most remarkable thing was that day was exactly one year after my father's death, and even more remarkable was that the number of votes on my name coincided exactly with the year of his birth. I felt so supported and embraced by him. For the first time, after a long time, I felt that he was taking care of me. Keep reading and you will understand what I mean.

SILENCE BEFORE THE STORM

I was born into a middle-class family in Mexico City. My parents were pioneers of Mexican television and that definitely influenced my choice to study communication sciences. From my mother, I inherited good manners, a love for politics, and a vocation to serve. From my father, I inherited a love of freedom, the art of conversation, and a business mentality.

I was educated under the strict discipline of the College of Salesian nuns, who with much effort taught me willpower, perseverance, and tenacity. Let me tell you, it was not easy for them to teach us. If there was a contest to see who gave more headaches to whom, I think the alumni would have won. My roots and my most valuable friendships are in that Salesian family. Together with my biological family, they gave me the great support that made it possible to live so far from my beloved Mexico.

I was a gymnast in the Y.M.C.A., where after many years of training, I won four national championships and was part of the national gymnastics team of the Mexican Olympic Committee (COM). Unfortunately, in 1984 we were informed that we would not go to the Los Angeles Olympics because there was no chance of winning medals. However, COM executives traveled there, representing the "organization." I was 14 years old then, and I learned the lesson that effort alone is not enough. You also need others to help you achieve your goals.

Shortly after that, I left gymnastics after breaking my ankle during an exercise on the balance beam. That was my favorite apparatus and my specialty. Since then, my life has been like walking on a thin beam, where the constant challenge is to balance and not to fall down.

I had a happy, carefree, and protected childhood. My father

had to travel a lot for his work and took us to places where we had never been, all over the world. We also had favorite places where we often spent time with each other. Those are moments of joy that every child should have. That calm and carefree life resembled the moment of tranquility and silence that precedes a devastating storm that destroys everything, leaving misfortune and desolation in its path.

My father suddenly became ill and our lives changed completely. He was never cured. He suffered from Alzheimer for 33 years of his life. A soul trapped in a body, unable to escape. At the age of 15, I was faced with being a student, an encyclopedia saleswoman, a caregiver, a psychologist, a social worker, and everything that was necessary to support the family situation.

Before I turned 18, I started working at IMEVISION (now TV Azteca) doing political programs, following advice from my father: "Know your country first, before going abroad." I traveled throughout Mexico, interviewing governors, politicians, and social activists. I always traveled with my books and studied with the faculty of political science at the National Autonomous University of Mexico (NAUM) on weekends. After school, I visited my father at the place where he interned. I turned 20 and studied two languages, worked full-time, and studied at the evening school. I combined what I had to do with what I really wanted to do to become the woman I am now.

Still, I thought *life, you don't owe me anything. Life, we are at peace.* My life is characterized by what destiny has in store for me, and also by what I decide to do with it. It is a parallel world where on one side I live and solve the problems that life presents to me, and on the other side, I build the life I want to have for myself. Does this mean life is effortless? No, sometimes it's very exhausting. With will and perseverance, you will get there, but everything is not in your own hands.

My father's sickness was a very sad and difficult time for my brother, my sisters, my mother, and me. When the end came, I was lucky to see my father before he died. The only thing that is fixed forever in my mind is his hand gripped tightly in mine, so that I wouldn't let it go, so that I wouldn't leave. As if he were clinging to life. But I had to take my plane back to Holland a couple of hours later. Even knowing that this would be the last time we would see each other in life, I had to separate our hands, give him the blessing and the last kiss, and leave the room with a broken heart. It was the most difficult moment of my entire life. Weeks later, papa would die, freeing himself from the useless body that had him imprisoned him for so long.

CHOOSING LOVE

Papa knew me very well, and it's like he seemed to know he'd get sick. He started to overload me with advice. He told me once, "You are born to choose, not to be chosen." And I have chosen to love.

For love, I left the family home. For love, I traveled to another country. For love, I had the most desired son in the world. For love, I have done the most crazy things you can imagine.

I have infinitely loved all my partners. And I have been very happy with them. But I also have a traveling soul, so when my family in Mexico was a little more stable, I left for Europe with what would be my handsome prince on a white horse. When they told me that my life would be like Cinderella's, they never told me that I would have to clean the crystal palace! The culture shock took a toll on our relationship. I had already left everything behind to adapt to another country, but I was not willing to lose my self-esteem.

When we separated, I decided to become an entrepreneur. I managed to spend more time with my son. That way I could personally help him with homework and look after his physical and mental well-being. I started as a Spanish teacher at the executive level. Those connections were the foundation of a network for my international trade and business development activities. Soon I travelled around the world, running diverse and interesting projects. I became a recognized businesswoman, a specialist in strategic communication. But above all, I became an independent woman. However, I never stopped supporting my parents in every way possible.

When I choose to forgive the people who hurt me and to value everyone for who they are, my life improved. That's because when you forgive, everything bad disappears. Whoever attacked you takes everything bad away with him. And he has to live with the fact that he was not able to beat you. He will see you get ahead and succeed in your purpose. So put yourself on a higher plane and from there you can use all your positivity and belief in yourself to forge your own success. Forgiving yourself is much more difficult to do, but if you do it and move on, there will be nothing to stop you. Be what you want to be; just do it!

SERVING IS GIVING

Every start has a finish. In 2008, I had to pay a heavy price for my many years of gymnastics. I was diagnosed with a double hernia in my spine that would change the course of my life completely, once again. Goodbye to airplanes, to long trips to distant countries, to long walks. Fortunately, at that time, my son was in high school, and I had more free time for myself.

One afternoon I was watching the news when I saw a politician who radiated that great "woman power" we always talk about. She inspired me to resume my political career. Her name was Rita Verdonk, a high-ranking minister in the Dutch government. So I made contact with her and participated in her political campaigns. Among other things, I helped her party to earn two seats on the council of the municipality in my city. My future would not be there, but for me that was the window that opened when other doors closed. I will always be grateful for the opportunity to rekindle my passion for politics again.

After that, I was invited to participate in the formation of a new political party called 50PLUS. The rest is history. This year we celebrated 10 years working together with others who think like me, trying to build a better country and a better Europe.

I believe everyone should learn from their own experiences and use whatever they can use in their favor. I believe that improving the world begins with improving ourselves. Everything that happens to us with our family and friends, our move to another country, our understanding and frustration, the underappreciation of our work and knowledge and our loneliness are only part of the wonderful opportunity that life gives us. It is all exercise to prepare us to receive what God has in store for us. Live life to the fullest extent of the word, "live."

By writing this book, I am celebrating my fiftieth anniversary. It's a perfect moment to look back at what I have achieved and to enjoy the life I've built around me: my partner, my son, my work, and my political ambitions to help people.

One thing is for sure. I will always keep moving forward.

REFLECTION QUESTIONS

1. What are you willing to risk to improve your situation?

2. What is it that prevents you from reaching your goals?

3. If you had the chance to realize one of your dreams, which one would you choose? What do you need to do or have to make it happen?

BIOGRAPHY

Adriana Hernández Martínez was born in 1969 and studied communication sciences at the National Autonomous University of Mexico (NAUM), specializing in politics. In 1987, she founded the broadcast television production company, Cirerol Comunicación, in Mexico. She managed the sales activities for 40 television stations in the country and produced political television programs. She was an advisor for provincial governments, members of parliament, and governors.

She moved to the Netherlands in 1996. There she taught Spanish language and business culture at Regina Coelli, one of the most renowned language institutes in Europe. In 2003, she founded the company, ArianMC as a culmination of the experience she had gained in international trade and business development, helping European, Asian, and Latin-American companies expand their business.

Since 2018, Adriana has served in the Municipal Council in the City of 's-Hertogenbosch in the Netherlands and as a board member of the Water Council Aa and Maas since 2015. She is a staff member for the Parliamentary faction in the European Parliament of her political Dutch party, 50PLUS.

Adriana Hernández Martínez
adriana.hernandez@50pluspartij.nl
Facebook: Adriana Hernandez 50PLUS

Renée Rodriguez

"We can not only create life, but live life creating!"

I lost the notion of time and dimension, but I could feel him. I knew exactly where he was. As I felt him descending, a wonderful white light covered me while I felt my body opening with an indescribable pleasure. I was in ecstasy! He was nearly here... and suddenly, he retreated.

I was in shock... I didn't know what happened. I felt defeated. I had been in such a "high and wonderful" state that I thought I couldn't possibly return. When I had reached that point with my first child, he simply slipped into the hands of his dad. This time, I was unsure whether I was going to be able to birth my child. For a few moments, I was in fear...

LINEAR TIMING AN ENEMY OF OUR INSTINCT

We were in the bathroom of our home in Belgium, the country where we moved only five months before. It was almost midnight. Our 3-year-old son had already fallen asleep. I was with two midwives and my husband, who was sitting nearby outside the bathtub where I was giving birth to our second child. About an hour before, he had been inside the bathtub with me and everything changed, along with the removal of a noisy clock from the room. That loud "tick tock" reminded me of the passing of linear time and unconsciously, listening to it was keeping me in this world, and mired within my control freak, hidden personality.

I wanted our baby to be born on March 21 for two reasons. First, I was told that if I had not started labor 24 hours after my water had broken, I would have to receive intravenous antibiotics to avoid the risk of infection. So, this meant that in a few hours, I might have to go to the hospital, which terrified me because I wanted to have a beautiful home birth like we did with our first child. The second reason for the desired March 21 date was because it was the Spring Equinox, a mystic day in Mexico, my home country. Now I know time limits and expectations are enemies of childbirth.

My water supposedly broke on March 21 at one o'clock in the morning, but the contractions didn't start, so I went back to sleep. The next morning, we enjoyed our last hours with our 3-year-old as the "only child." We went for a lovely walk in the forest. It was one of the first "warm" days after a cold winter in Belgium. As a Latina coming from Cuernavaca, the city of Eternal Spring in Mexico, I must admit that the cold, dark, European winters are a challenge. However, I learned to appreciate every season in the same way I learned to enjoy living in different countries. But that day, deep inside, there was a sadness in my heart. I felt nostalgic about giving birth so far away from my home and family. I know Latinas understand this feeling.

Labor would have to start before midnight to avoid going to the hospital where I might be induced with synthetic oxytocin, intervention I'm against since we women can, and shall produce natural oxytocin. So, I want to share what has made both of my births not only pleasurable, but even orgasmic. As part of my mission to help women exchange pain for pleasure, I must talk about this. I want to tell the new generation of moms and give them the choice to accept it. I want to reveal the secret rather than have it remain a taboo, or even a myth!

THE ROLE OF FEMALE ORGASM IN LABOR

What am I talking about? The role of the female orgasm in labor! It's unbelievable that with the advancements in science, we still know so little about the female orgasm. One of its functions, among many other joyful ones, is to give birth faster and with pleasure, thanks to the release of the hormone of love: oxytocin. Its Greek etymology means "quick childbirth." So yes, we women are physically designed to conceive and give birth with pleasure, even in ecstasy. Unfortunately, society and religion have mentally designed women to conceive, give birth, and live with pressure and pain, totally disconnected from their bodies, emotions, and instincts.

So at five o'clock that evening, my husband and I had decided to "naturally induce" labor by making love, which goes beyond "having sex" or penetration (which should be avoided after water breaks). Making love goes beyond the body. It's truly connecting, not only on the physical level, but in the spiritual one, where through caresses, touch, and physical sensations, we connect soul to soul. Where there is no "goal" for instant pleasure, but both are truly present in the sensations, the emotions. Just feeling and enjoying the present moment without rushing, without aiming for something.

Without being selfish, I let both of us concentrate on me, on my pleasure and my desires. I asked my husband what I wanted: "scratch my bony back," "massage my lower back" and "give me a "fast and furious orgasm." That's what I call a clitoral orgasm that I easily reach, which is truly releasing, but not as powerful as other types of orgasms. However, during labor, it has magic effects and you can reach it with your partner or by yourself.

Thus, after this deep, beautiful, and releasing sexual connection with orgasm, I felt a beautiful flow of natural oxytocin through my body and my contractions started! With every contraction, I took a deep breath and instinctively, with my mouth wide open, I let the breath out while singing "Aaaaaaaaaaaa." The contraction will fade along with the sound, leaving me with a peaceful sensation and making each contraction beautiful and powerful, but not painful. I was truly amazed by the fact that I didn't feel "pain" during any of my labors. They were definitely both intense and powerful, but at the same time, truly pleasurable. Then why is giving birth often painful?

Any mammal, including humans in labor, by feeling observed, having a lack of privacy, in a strange environment with bright lights, might unconsciously feel threatened and trigger the "fight or flight" reaction. The body produces stress hormones, like adrenaline and cortisol, to stop labor and flee to a place where the mother feels safe enough to give birth.

Fear paralyzes us, even in birthing. If we don't fight or flee our fears, they get stuck in our body and become painful. If we are fearful and under the effect of adrenaline and stress when giving birth, our body, and mainly the cervix, gets tight and rigid, so labor becomes unbearably painful and slows down. This leads to medical interventions, and very likely, complications which make the experience painful and traumatic, instead of beautiful and transforming.

Pregnancy is not only a perfect time to work with your fears, it's the TIME to do it. Work to release whatever is hurting you, painful, or limiting you, and allow yourself to be free and light, to flow and enjoy. A new baby will be born, but also, a new woman. Drop the backpack with the old and heavy stones so you can step into motherhood feeling lighter, with strength and space to face the coming challenges joyfully and courageously.

TRUST, SURRENDER AND LET GO

After three hours of being in and out of the bath, moving, dancing, and apparently flowing, I could feel I was not there yet. The big loud clock was reminding me that the time to go to the hospital was approaching.

Finally, I allowed myself to recognize that I was in fear. I called my midwife and told her I was worried because I didn't feel I was in "real" labor, but I was pushing myself to start. Just admitting my feelings made me feel much better. For the first time, she did a vaginal examination, and we found out that my water had not completely broken but had only torn on the top. She looked into my eyes and with a lovely voice told me, "Don't worry, your baby is still protected; we don't have to go to the hospital in two hours. You have all the time you want, and I will be here whenever your baby is ready!"

I asked her to remove the clock and to bring my husband back. And then, with no timing, with no limits, I connected with my husband and let myself go. Thanks to his kissing and sensual touch, the oxytocin came back and the contractions started again, this time, very powerfully. I stopped guiding my body and let it guide me. Suddenly my body started moving like a cow-cat yoga movement and I felt a strong "PUM." My water broke and I crossed the veil to another dimension.

I felt strong but light, powerful but sensitive, a feline, a mammal, me in my full expression... until the moment I reached an incredible ecstasy, but my baby didn't come out...

"He was almost here... I don't know what happened," I said in despair.

My midwife, with her tender and soft voice replied, "You are doing great. It's amazingly beautiful to see you birthing with a smile. Don't worry, he will come when it is time."

The words of my midwife gave me the support I needed. I felt understood, empowered, and capable. So I closed my eyes again and let my instinctive wisdom guide me. I entered into a trance again. My husband tried to touch me to comfort me, but I refused. I needed my space; I needed to reconnect with my inner power, with myself. I knew my husband and my midwives were there; I could feel them and totally trusted them. Therefore, I no longer needed touch or comforting words. I just needed silence and trust.

ORGASMIC BIRTH

Suddenly, my body got into its desired position, kneeling inside the bath with one knee on the floor and the other bent. The beautiful, white light started appearing again and intensifying while rising. I could feel my baby going down the birth channel and my body opening with a divine pleasure. Without force, my body instinctively pushed, a powerful, yet gentle push... I felt his head emerging and I reached out to him with my hands. I could see and feel his head under the water, but his body was still inside me. He challenged me again. I took a profound breath; I felt the last magnificent and powerful contraction. I held my breath while feeling my baby going out of my body into this world. I was in a complete ecstasy. I took him and put him to my breast. This was the most divine experience I ever had.

Xander was born eleven minutes after midnight on March 22-- not the day I wanted, but the day he chose. Not the way I imagined, but beyond my expectations.

I was amazed to experience how beautiful, empowering, and even orgasmic giving birth could be. My two childbirths were so transforming for me that I found my mission in life: to inspire and guide women to have orgasmic births and pleasurable lives. I feel a calling to tell my story to inspire more women to give themselves the possibility of birth with pleasure and understand childbirth as a journey of transformation instead of focusing on the pain. That's how I stepped out of my fears, left my previous, stressful career and gave birth to a meaningful company called "Momfulness. life."

I believe the way we give birth and the way we are born will influence our lives forever. So it's time to reclaim our power, to reconnect ourselves with the inner wisdom of our magic bodies and change pain for pleasure and fear for love, not only when giving birth but when living. Let's learn to connect with our sexual energy and our multi-orgasmic potential so we can not only create life, but live life creating!

REFLECTION QUESTIONS

1. If you already gave birth. How was the experience? If it was painful, can you identify the real "pain or fear" behind the situation? In most cases the pain is cause for the disconnection – not in that moment, but through our lives - with our body and our own sexuality, a trauma that we are holding, which can be a sexual trauma or something related with the masculine. Talk to your womb to find the reason behind the pain.

2. What comes to your mind when you hear the word "pleasure." Do you allow yourself to feel pleasure, not only in sex, but in life, in living, in being?

3. If you are not yet a mother and would like to be, would you like to have an orgasmic birth? The way we birth is the way we live, so start having an orgasmic life where you feel connected with your body, your emotions, your spirituality, and your pleasure.

BIOGRAPHY

Renée Rodriguez is a Mexican mother and businesswoman. Ranking first in her class, she earned her M.S. in Management in France from KEDGE Business School and from the Hong Kong University of Science and Technology. She is a business advisor for Latin American companies seeking commerce with China.

Renée co-founded MEXCHAM, the Mexican Chamber of Commerce in Hong Kong. She also partnered with an accounting firm in Hong Kong to open a representative office in Mexico and became partner and director of the Iberoamerican Department.

The beautiful, transformational births of her sons created her life purpose: to inspire and guide women to have orgasmic lives and orgasmic births. Renée believes the way we are born and give birth defines our life, and she can best contribute to the world by changing painful births to orgasmic ones. She created the company "Momfulness life", to inspire the new generation of moms to give birth in pleasure and love, not fear and pain. She also helps women connect with their sexual energy and their multi-orgasmic potential so they can access their inner power and give birth orgasmically to whatever they want, not only children.

Renée Rodriguez
www.momfulness.life
Facebook: Momfulness.life

Made in the
USA
Monee, IL